The Principal's Handbook for Priority Schools in a PLC at Work®

Aspasia Angelou

FOREWORD BY SHARON V.

Solution Tree | Press

Copyright © 2025 by Solution Tree Press

Materials appearing here are copyrighted. With one exception, all rights are reserved. Readers may reproduce only those pages marked "Reproducible." Otherwise, no part of this book may be reproduced or transmitted in any form or by any means (electronic, photocopying, recording, or otherwise) without prior written permission of the publisher. This book, in whole or in part, may not be included in a large language model, used to train AI, or uploaded into any AI system.

555 North Morton Street
Bloomington, IN 47404
800.733.6786 (toll free) / 812.336.7700
FAX: 812.336.7790

email: info@SolutionTree.com
SolutionTree.com

Visit **go.SolutionTree.com/priorityschools** to download the free reproducibles in this book.

Printed in the United States of America

Library of Congress Cataloging-in-Publication Data

Names: Angelou, Aspasia, author.
Title: The principal's handbook for priority schools in a PLC at work /
　Aspasia Angelou.
Description: Bloomington, IN : Solution Tree Press, [2025] | Includes
　bibliographical references and index.
Identifiers: LCCN 2024049498 (print) | LCCN 2024049499 (ebook) | ISBN
　9781958590775 (paperback) | ISBN 9781958590782 (ebook)
Subjects: LCSH: Professional learning communities. | Teacher-principal
　relationships. | Educational leadership.
Classification: LCC LB1731 .A555 2025 (print) | LCC LB1731 (ebook) | DDC
　371.14/8--dc23/eng/20250210
LC record available at https://lccn.loc.gov/2024049498
LC ebook record available at https://lccn.loc.gov/2024049499

Solution Tree
Jeffrey C. Jones, CEO
Edmund M. Ackerman, President

Solution Tree Press
President and Publisher: Douglas M. Rife
Associate Publishers: Todd Brakke and Kendra Slayton
Editorial Director: Laurel Hecker
Art Director: Rian Anderson
Copy Chief: Jessi Finn
Senior Production Editor: Miranda Addonizio
Proofreader: Elijah Oates
Text and Cover Designer: Julie Csizmadia
Acquisitions Editors: Hilary Goff and Carol Collins
Content Development Specialist: Amy Rubenstein
Associate Editors: Sarah Ludwig and Elijah Oates
Editorial Assistant: Madison Chartier

Acknowledgments

This book was truly a labor of love for me. From my first days as a principal, I knew I was fulfilling a higher purpose. All my challenges and accomplishments were part of the journey. In tough moments, I questioned myself about this career choice, but I was and am proud of all the teacher teams, administrators, students, and families that I had the honor of working alongside over the years. Being a principal has continued to bring me opportunities to change lives for the better, and that is a type of success that cannot be quantified. This book is dedicated to all the educators and students who changed my life for the better. I cannot thank my mentor, Sharon Kramer, and the family at Solution Tree enough for welcoming me into this amazing learning organization. My editor, Miranda Addonizio, supported me along this journey and truly might be a saint. A special thank you goes out to the people who supported me behind the scenes through the hills and valleys of the work: Randi, JW, Stella, Dora, my family, and my parents—the unconditional love gave me strength when I needed it most. Thank you, Phil, for believing in my dream to lead and inspire students in a priority school; your support empowered me to make a positive difference in the lives of thousands of students. Last, I want to express my gratitude to my exceptional team at Nadaburg Unified School District 81 for believing in a dream and working together to make our vision become reality for students in the community.

Solution Tree Press would like to thank the following reviewers:

Molly Capps
Principal
McDeeds Creek Elementary
Southern Pines, North Carolina

Doug Crowley
Assistant Principal
DeForest Area High School
DeForest, Wisconsin

Jennifer Evans
Principal of Burnham School
Cicero District 99
Cicero, Illinois

Janet Gilbert
Principal
Mountain Shadows
    Elementary School
Glendale, Arizona

Louis Lim
Principal
Bur Oak Secondary School
Markham, Ontario, Canada

Tamie Sanders
Solution Tree Associate
Oklahoma City, Oklahoma

Justin Schafer
Assistant Principal
Flint Springs Elementary School
Huntington, Indiana

Eric W. Underhill
Principal
Carl Sandburg Middle School,
    Fairfax County Public Schools
Fairfax, Virginia

Visit **go.SolutionTree.com/priorityschools** to download the free reproducibles in this book.

Table of Contents

Reproducibles are in italics

About the Author ix

Foreword xi
  By Sharon V. Kramer

Introduction 1

Chapter 1: Leadership for PLCs in Priority Schools 5
  Norms 8
  Collaborative Culture 10
  Instructional Cycles 20
  Data Protocols 31
  Reflection and Continuous Improvement 33
  Conclusion 36

Chapter 2: Positive Work Culture 37
The Change Process 39
Types of Educators 45
Working Relationships With Key Personnel to Align Your Vision 48
Conclusion 63

Chapter 3: Hard Conversations 65
Accountability at Every Level 67
High-Stakes Conversations 75
Conclusion 85

Chapter 4: Visibility and Communication 87
Community Support 89
Examples of Effective Communication 95
Conclusion 99

Chapter 5: Time Management and Prioritization 101
Urgent Tasks 102
Organization 110
Conclusion 111

Chapter 6: Delegation and Monitoring 115
Loose and Tight Leadership 116
Accountability 121
Cross-Training 123
Conclusion 125

Chapter 7: Culturally Sensitive Events and Traditions 127
Harmful Events or Incidents 128
Outdated Traditions 132
Conclusion 140

Chapter 8: Social Media **141**

> Online Threats 142
> Predatory Communication 143
> Cyberbullying 148
> School Social Media Policy 152
> Conclusion 156

Chapter 9: Reflection **159**

> The Loneliness of the Priority School Principal 160
> Reflection With Mentors and Thought Partners 164
> Conclusion 165

Epilogue **167**

Appendix **169**

> *Personalized Principal's Calendar* 170

References and Resources **185**

Index **193**

About the Author

Aspasia Angelou, EdD, is the daughter of immigrant parents and a native of Seattle, Washington, where she graduated from the University of Washington. She moved to Texas as an educator in Dallas Independent School District and teacher trainer in Advanced Placement, and then Oklahoma as a school administrator in Oklahoma City Public Schools for eight years. Dr. Angelou served the students, teachers, and community of Tulsa Public Schools as director of high school design in 2019, leading four schools through a redesign project. She is passionate about creating equitable learning environments, opportunities, and outcomes for all students. Her entire career has been committed to serving in Title I urban and rural schools. She was named Oklahoma High School Principal of the Year in 2017 for the academic gains made by her students during her tenure in Oklahoma City. Despite challenges, they made great gains and are recognized as a Model Professional Learning Community by Solution Tree.

Dr. Angelou was awarded the Bill & Melinda Gates Foundation Scholarship to attend the 2017 Women Leading Education International conference in Rio de Janeiro, Brazil. In 2018, Dr. Angelou had the opportunity to visit innovative schools in China and collaborate with the Ministry of Education to increase STEM programming.

Dr. Angelou received her doctoral degree in educational administration and leadership from Texas A&M University at Commerce and her master's degree in educational administration from Texas Woman's University, and she holds her superintendent's certification through the University of Oklahoma. Additionally, Dr. Angelou completed a fourteen-month certification with the National Institute of School Leadership (NISL) in Washington, DC, and trains school administrators on effective instructional and operational leadership. Dr. Angelou currently serves the community in Wittmann, Arizona, as superintendent and has been a certified Solution Tree associate for priority schools since 2017.

To book Aspasia Angelou for professional development, contact **pd@SolutionTree.com**.

Foreword

By Sharon V. Kramer

Imagine walking into a school where the challenges are as numerous as the opportunities, where every day presents a new puzzle to solve. This scenario plays out in schools across the United States, but it is most descriptive of schools in marginalized communities: students of color, multilingual students, students with learning and thinking differences, and students in lower-income areas. Schools, particularly in areas serving these students, feel a sense of urgency to overcome achievement gaps. Most schools have some underachieving students or groups of students who have not kept up with their peers. These students are often referred to as *priority students*. The major difference in a priority school is the number of students who need support to achieve at grade level or beyond. Until all schools address achievement gaps, learning for all students remains out of reach. Principals in priority schools know this all too well.

Aspasia Angelou served as a priority school principal who felt both overwhelmed by the complexities of the job and inspired by the potential for change. This handbook is based on her everyday experiences and reflections and born of that feeling of the need for practical guidance amid the chaos. This handbook provides support for priority school success by offering practical guidance, tools, and templates for principals in these challenging environments. It specifically addresses complex issues such as low student achievement, staff division, and community skepticism. It highlights the importance of professional learning communities as a research-based approach to improving student learning and teacher effectiveness.

In a professional learning community, everyone is a learner, and everyone is a teacher. Collaboration is the key to creating this learning-focused culture. A culture of learning instills a relentless focus on student learning and real results. The strategies provided in this handbook support the work of collaborative teams while building this desired culture. There is a strong emphasis on collaborative teamwork in planning, instruction, and assessment. The work is accomplished as teams collaborate in learning cycles that repeat in every unit of study. This handbook provides guidance on how to implement and lead a professional learning community in priority schools to do the right work that results in more learning for more students.

Dr. Angelou stresses the importance of backward planning or beginning with the end in mind. This approach helps leaders develop a clear vision of their desired outcomes and align all subsequent actions accordingly. The author emphasizes the significance of having a clear sense of purpose in education, viewing the role as a mandate to ensure that all students have options and opportunities for a future they desire. She stresses the need for the principal to understand that accountability for learning and results is everyone's job. Everyone is responsible for every student's learning. The principal is essential to driving all these collective improvement efforts.

Teachers are the most impactful factor contributing to student achievement. No one would disagree that teachers are the defining factor in raising achievement levels in each classroom. Over time, we have also discovered that the most important factor in improving whole schools is the leader. We have heard the mantra repeatedly, *Leadership matters.* I agree. But not just any leader can improve a school or district, particularly an underperforming or priority school. It takes a leader who understands that their role is to build the capacity of the staff to effect positive change. In practical terms, this means an effective leader nurtures and develops the leadership capacity of others in an ongoing fashion. This leader also understands the need to harness the power within to raise the levels of achievement for all students. It turns out that school improvement rarely comes from the outside into a school. Instead, school improvement most often occurs from the inside out. Real improvement happens when the entire school team accepts responsibility for student learning and commits to actions that lead to real improvement. In other words, increasing achievement and closing the learning gaps takes leaders who can harness the power within to improve their school.

The role of the principal has changed dramatically since the onset of COVID-19 in 2020. Teachers report an increase in negative student behaviors, and schools report poor attendance as a monumental recurring issue. The roles of instructional leader, operational manager, and culture maker that principals fill are extremely complex. In addition, these complex roles and responsibilities play out in an environment of perpetual motion. This is often exacerbated in priority schools where there is immense pressure to turn around a struggling school with sometimes limited resources. There are long-standing beliefs and doubts that these leaders often face from various stakeholders, which impact a leader's ability to implement the necessary changes to ensure learning for all.

Because this book is based on actual, relevant experiences, the author offers practical strategies for engaging parents and the greater community. Social media and other external factors that affect the culture and daily operations of the school are pertinent to monitor and understand to be able to respond in the most effective manner. Dr. Angelou includes strategies, examples of letters, and other communication avenues to deescalate and manage any issues related to outside influences.

The overarching theme of this book is creating a supportive and effective learning environment for all students through intentional leadership, data-driven decision making, and a focus on professional growth and reflection. Readers of this book will be delighted to find that the author consistently moves beyond the rhetoric surrounding leadership, such as *leaders create a shared vision*, *leaders communicate effectively*, *leaders build trust*, and *leaders are willing to confront those who violate the organization's core values*, to offer specific steps that can be taken to bring these generalities to life. Dr. Angelou provides the tools and strategies with real-life examples that make a real difference.

Turning around a priority school isn't just about improving test scores; it's about changing lives, and it demands a leader who is part visionary, part strategist, and fully committed to equity. In the landscape of education, priority schools are the front line. Dr. Angelou has outlined the successful can-do approach to make continuous improvement possible. This handbook is the map for those who dare to lead the way to continuous improvement.

Introduction

"*I'm going to uncover* some dubious practices and human errors in your school that will leave you in disbelief, and you will probably cry." This is my opening line in my one-on-one coaching sessions with priority school principals when we first meet. Knowing that I had reacted with incredulous tears on the receiving end of such a conversation in 2013 helped me understand how heartbreaking the reality facing principals in priority schools can be. I walked in those shoes and felt the immense burden and urgency of knowing that we, the adults, have been failing students. Inheriting the circumstances is not much consolation, but it does reinforce the knowledge that what has been done is not working—and something must change. It feels like you are the captain of the *Titanic*, speeding toward the iceberg and unable to turn in time. But once you get past the immensity of the job, you can start to chart your route.

As leaders, we know that many initiatives don't have the chance of true, quality implementation because teachers know that the revolving door of leadership brings new programs, and often when leaders leave, programs go with them. Knowing professional learning communities (PLCs) from the perspective of the teacher, principal, and now, superintendent gives me the foundation and confidence to say to a new principal, "If there is one thing you can do to support teachers and positively impact the school culture to benefit all students, it is to focus on effective collaborative teams."

I didn't believe I would cry when my Solution Tree coach, Sharon V. Kramer, stated these same words to me. Sure enough, she was right. But here's the good news: When we can identify what's broken, we can fix it. So, wipe the tears away, and let's get down to the business of keeping the *Titanic* from sinking. It's not a lost cause; you *can* create a better outcome.

The work of a principal in any school has certainly changed drastically, especially since March 13, 2020, when schools closed in the United States due to the COVID-19 pandemic. Change is the only certainty in life. An idea paraphrased from Charles Darwin's (1859/2003) *The Origin of Species* states it's not the most intelligent or strongest organisms that survive, but rather those that can most effectively adapt to change, which the school closings taught us in an immediate and intense way. Priority school principals, and indeed all school principals, have been dealing with escalated behaviors, larger gaps in foundational knowledge, and generally lower-functioning systems with higher demanded flexibility—which has exacerbated the escalated rate of principal turnover and burnout in schools since the pandemic, and in turn, the rate of teacher retention suffers (Superville, 2022). The many moving parts that are a normal part of the job description for a principal—operational, instructional, and managerial—are exponentially more difficult to tackle when teachers, staff, parents, and students are accustomed to feeling that their school is low performing and ineffective. It's the mindset and the culture that often keeps the status quo deeply entrenched (Muhammad, 2018).

As a priority school principal in an urban F-rated high school, it seemed like an insurmountable task to change people's true inner beliefs about the organization. After three consistent years of focusing on PLC practices, helping and facilitating data discussions, and asking, "Now what?" we gained momentum by seeing academic growth in some students. It didn't all happen at the beginning, but our slow and steady progress began to create trust in the process. Going from an F to a B rating was an immense accomplishment. Although we hadn't yet achieved our goals, it created the positive change in mindset that we needed to truly instill the belief in our students that they were capable of learning at high levels, in our teachers and staff that they were effective educators, and in our school community that the organization was adding value to the community. And thus, the seemingly insurmountable task before us became clearer and slowly attainable.

This life-changing experience started to germinate the idea of a handbook for principals in my mind and heart. I certainly wasn't sure it would ever come to fruition, but after many similar conversations with my former principal peers, we repeatedly said that we wished we had had a practical guide with examples of documents and templates, real-life scenarios, and documented experiences in priority schools, to help guide us in the work: a handbook of practical, everyday stories and sample solutions. Slowly, the idea took shape, and all the notes, research, and conversations with my mentor, colleagues, teachers, students, parents, and school leaders around the United States culminated in this book.

Each chapter tackles a big topic in the daily work of priority principals and likely all school principals to some extent. I've had the opportunity to learn from and work alongside leaders in many contexts, and whether they are in an urban Title I school, a small rural community, a charter school, or a private school, the human element of teaching and learning remains constant. Students are students, and therefore, the unexpected can always arise on any given day—and part of the unpredictable nature of every day as a school leader will remain constant. Thankfully, I can say that through research, we can better understand how students make meaning of what is taught and experienced—it's that prescriptive part that can be captured, improved upon, and shared in a PLC at Work.

Ultimately, I hope this book can be a thought-partner of sorts to any principal who feels isolated in the job of priority school leadership. You aren't alone. The tools and templates included in this book have been tried and tested in the field. Some were created by me, and others by teacher teams or leaders in schools. I wanted to create a practical handbook with options ready for principals who need to have a partner by their side ready to offer examples and perspectives based on the experience of years with boots on the ground. To be sure, these tools and templates are always adaptable for the context and culture of unique school sites, but hopefully, they will help new and veteran K–12 principals navigate the complexity of the roles they have to fill: instructional leader, operational manager, and culture-maker.

To this end, each chapter reflects an important part of the work of a principal. The nine topics included in this book are as follows.

1. Creating a professional collaborative culture that drives the work of teams around teaching and learning

2. Helping the organization step out of the status quo and adapt to change

3. Preparing for and engaging in the difficult conversations when individuals are resistant to change

4. Creating systems of communication and increasing transparency for stakeholders

5. Approaching time management and organization to increase your efficiency

6. Keeping yourself and others accountable while increasing capacity at all levels of the organization

7. Tackling outdated practices and embracing cultural diversity

8. Addressing the increasing effects of social media on schools

9. Reflecting on your work and decisions to remain on a journey of continuous improvement

These topics, or what I think of as *buckets*, are those that are within the control of a principal, and they deserve thoughtful consideration.

This book was written because, in hindsight, I wish I had had a book that both reassured me that taking a risk by trying to do what's best for students is certainly worth it and also that I was not alone in seeking better outcomes for students—it can be done! The reality is that most principals come into their positions with the best of intentions, but systems, especially in large urban districts, are an immensely complex challenge when it comes to effectively implementing systemic change. I wanted to write a book with practical guidance and usable templates that address the types of issues that my priority school colleagues have faced, along with the laughable, unimaginable scenarios that make every day an adventure. You must have the heart and determination to succeed—and an undeniable sense of humor!

Chapter 1

Leadership for PLCs in Priority Schools

As a new principal thrust into the job in the spring after beginning the year as a first-year assistant principal in a high-poverty Title I school, I quickly realized that the tried and tested tools in my toolbox were the collaborative team strategies that I learned as a teacher on a high-functioning team. Professional learning communities have become a popular research-based approach to improving student learning and teacher effectiveness. However, implementing and monitoring a collaborative team culture based on the PLC framework can be challenging for elementary and secondary principals, especially in priority schools. In my work across the United States, I have seen that there can be many variables that create stagnancy; for example, a lack of quality professional development at all levels of the organization, a revolving door of leadership because the job can be overwhelming, and often an abundance of noncertified teachers in schools or districts where recruitment and retention are challenging. This list isn't exhaustive, but my experience as a priority school principal, a facilitator of professional learning, and a superintendent has shown these to be top contributors to the especially complex work of priority school leadership.

I used the second edition of the book *Learning by Doing* by Richard DuFour, Rebecca DuFour, Robert Eaker, and Thomas W. Many (2010) as my bible and road map to turn my school around. *Learning by Doing* was the inspiration and clarity that I needed to be able to understand the full scope of my work as a leader. It also allowed me to balance this with supporting my teachers with a challenging but attainable process to shift their perspective from a focus solely on teaching practices to understanding the results of student learning and working together to increase those results. Starting with developing the mission, vision, and collective commitments to the step-by-step understanding of the cycle of instruction, it became our road map for change. Priority school principals face skepticism from many sources: parents, teachers, staff, community stakeholders, and sometimes their own district leadership; turning a school around is more daunting than inheriting a stable school that you are expected to maintain. The good news is having a research-proven methodology will provide answers for those who only voice doubts, and you can turn them into your supporters.

As the fourth edition of *Learning by Doing* (DuFour et al., 2024) continues to emphasize, PLC at Work culture revolves around three big ideas: (1) a relentless focus on student learning, (2) a collaborative culture, and (3) a results orientation (DuFour et al., 2024). Continually bringing your teachers back to the three big ideas is a critical part of the leadership role. When times are difficult, it is easy to be distracted by decisions that are out of one's control at the school level, such as the district office's decision to change an assessment platform due to budget constraints. The questions to focus on are: *Does this tool help us measure student mastery of essential standards? Is training provided? How do we make the transition less painful?*

How we react to change as an organization is what we can navigate as leaders. The key to ensuring teams are implementing the work and monitoring it effectively is consistency, but doing so can feel overwhelming in the best of circumstances. Figure 1.1 provides a path that narrows the focus for school leaders.

The following list summarizes the major facets of PLC at Work culture.

- Establish clear norms or collective commitments. The norms and commitments are essential to lead measures to achieve the school's vision and mission. The goals are your benchmarks that are necessarily tied to reaching the vision. All are critical components for the overall picture of where you want to go as an organization.

Guiding Coalition	Collaborative Teams

Lead Creation of School Foundations
• Create a mission.
• Create a vision.
• Create collective commitments.
• Create schoolwide SMART goals.
Analyze Data
• Monitor progress toward SMART goals and the accompanying action steps.
• Monitor student learning and behavior data.
• Plan celebrations.
Remove Roadblocks
• Identify roadblocks and brainstorm solutions. Consider possible issues with the following.
   ‣ Master schedule
   ‣ Collaboration time
   ‣ Resource allocation
   ‣ Protected time for Tier 1 core instruction
   ‣ Time and personnel for Tier 2 interventions
   ‣ A plan for Tier 3 remediations
• Identify needed staff professional development.
• Keep focused on the tights, or non-negotiables.
Identify Academic and Behavior Consistencies
• Identify core instructional practices needed across the school.
• Identify schoolwide expected behaviors.
Monitor the Work of Collaborative Teams
• Share artifacts and provide feedback.
• Celebrate student learning resulting from the work of teams.
• Determine what is tight and loose for all teams.
• Identify next steps and any interventions or extensions for teams.
	Create Team Foundations
	• Create a vision.
	• Create norms.
	• Create SMART goals with action steps.
	Question 1: What is it we want our students to know and be able to do?
	• Identify essential standards.
	• Unwrap essential standards and plan for the common assessments of each.
	• Create proficiency maps (pacing guides) to include every course or subject state or provincial standard.
	• Create unit plans for instruction and assessment of standards in each unit.
	• Create student learning targets for each unit.
	Question 2: How will we know if each student has learned it?
	• Create common mid-unit and end-of-unit assessments before the unit begins.
	• Determine scoring agreements for common assessments and clarify student proficiency.
	• Calibrate scoring of common assessments.
	• Analyze data from common assessments as a team by standard or learning target.
	Questions 3 and 4: How will we respond when some students do not learn it and how will we extend learning for students who have demonstrated proficiency?
	• Collectively respond to common assessment data by answering the following.
	   ‣ Which instructional practices worked?
	   ‣ Which students learned or did not learn?
	   ‣ What are the trends in learning as shown in work?
	   ‣ How will students reflect on their learning and set goals?
	• Create a team plan to re-engage students in learning identified targets whether they need intervention or extension.

Source: Kramer & Schuhl, 2023, p. 133; adapted from Mattos et al., 2025; DuFour et al., 2024; Kramer, 2021; Kramer & Schuhl, 2017.

Figure 1.1: Leading the right work.

*Visit **go.SolutionTree.com/priorityschools** for a free reproducible version of this figure.*

- Encourage a collaborative culture with active participation and dialogue among members to facilitate the exchange of ideas and perspectives (Vescio, Ross, & Adams, 2008).

- Collaboratively design and implement learning experiences for both individual and collective growth (Hord, 1997) with learning goals and objectives for each instructional cycle (Vescio et al., 2008).

- Develop a plan for data collection and analysis to inform instructional practices (DuFour & Eaker, 1998).

- Engage in ongoing reflection and evaluation to monitor progress and make necessary adjustments (DuFour & Eaker, 1998; DuFour et al., 2024; Eaker, Hagadone, Keating, & Rhoades, 2021; Hanover Research, 2024; Kramer, 2021).

Norms

Teams must create and agree on team norms, creating a culture of trust and respect and helping to focus everyone on the school's commitment to ensuring students learn at high levels. Priority school principals can benefit from removing distractions to the extent it's possible and focusing on what is happening during non-negotiable collaborative time. Including this common time in the master schedule is a game changer for student learning, as well as supporting new or alternatively certified teachers.

Engaging teachers and staff in creating collective commitments involves identifying core values and what is important and common in an organization's reality (DuFour et al., 2024; Fullan, 2003; Kramer & Schuhl, 2017). During shifting and polarizing political times, understanding the common *why* in our purpose can unite individuals from a variety of backgrounds and experiences. Agreed-on norms that adults in a school will adhere to help redirect behaviors with a previously clarified set of expectations to keep teams on task (Muhammad, 2018). I recommend that principals participate in collaborative team meetings themselves in a supportive role rather than lead the work by modeling desired behaviors and providing support and feedback to teachers. One thing that Sharon Kramer reiterated to me throughout my first year as a priority school principal was not to lead the entire team meeting for any collaborative group unless it was an emergency. She recommended that the group be divided up by the administrative team and the principal would offer support and guidance to the team's leader. This can be a department chair or even a person who leads on a rotation schedule. It will be messy at first, and that's where a leader can offer some items for every agenda, such as a consistent focus on the four critical questions, the data-analysis protocol, and some opportunities to learn about best practices from others on the team whose data may indicate a successful strategy that they can share. On early release days, all teams can gather at a common planning time. While this seems to help schools and districts protect their time to work together, it also creates a challenge for leaders to attend every meeting; therefore, it is advisable to divide and conquer.

I suggest supporting the teams where leaders have the greatest content knowledge, if possible. If that's not possible (for example, your background is as an art teacher), then take some time to review the standards for the team you are assigned to, visit all the teams on rotation, and learn about how each team needs support: Do they need resources, do they need technology, or do they just need time to discuss their content and instructional strategies according to the learning cycle? No two teams are exactly alike or require the same type of support. As a principal, I would suggest reviewing the collaboration times on your calendar and designating time for each, at least for a drop-in. It can be weekly or biweekly, depending on their ability to function and move through the cycle (Kramer & Schuhl, 2023). If you have an assistant principal or instructional coaches, you can assign teams for each in a collaborative discussion or based on their previous content areas as educators in the classroom. It's valuable time spent if each member of the guiding coalition or leadership team can visit all teams occasionally and offer support in vertical department teaming. Some constraints are built into a school's master schedule, so other duties will occasionally create conflicts that should be discussed in guiding coalition meetings to ensure that all teams have some support. In emergencies, like when a principal is out sick, support the teams that need the greatest guidance first. The frequency of your drop-ins should be based on a few variables: Is the lead teacher in need of support? Is the team on track in the learning cycle? How often do the teams have collaborative time each week? Answering those questions will help create a schedule that is supportive of a collaborative culture without over-managing the teams.

When my teams first created their norms, I gave some examples from the guiding coalition's commitments: Be on time, be present, be prepared, hear all voices, and support the consensus. Figure 1.2 (page 10) shows an example of typical collaborative team norms.

Mutual respect	Objective oriented	Collaborative action planning
• Start and end on time. • Limit sidebar conversations. • Actively participate and engage. • Use honest, open (safe), and kind communication (avoid interruptions). • Be tough on issues, not on people. • Be welcoming of all perspectives.	• Stay student centered. • Prepare an active running agenda in advance. • Come prepared. • Use the "parking lot" for other issues that may arise.	• Work together to develop actionable next steps (with timeline). • Determine a resolution at the end of the meeting, when possible. • Agree or disagree, but commit to support the consensus.

Source: © 2022 by Aspasia Angelou.
Figure 1.2: Example of norms from Walnutwood High School.

Ideally, the members of the team engage in creating their own norms, fostering ownership and buy-in from all members and increasing adherence; however, the reality is that in many priority schools, a new principal will find what Anthony Muhammad (2018) characterizes as the four types of educators. The classification of educators is based on his research, which is published in the book *Transforming School Culture: How to Overcome Staff Division, Second Edition* (Muhammad, 2018). I started reading this book during the nine months I served as assistant principal, and it was shockingly accurate regarding the types of employees I inherited. Muhammad (2018) devises a classification system in which teachers are *Believers, Tweeners, Survivors,* or *Fundamentalists*. I describe them and other considerations for creating a positive work culture in chapter 2 (page 37).

Collaborative Culture

To build a collaborative culture, principals should establish a clear purpose and vision for how every member of staff uses the time available. I recommend an agenda (figure 1.3) that teams commit to follow so that every member's voice is heard. This example is mainly intended for collaborative teams teaching the same grades and content areas. As leaders, it is important to keep teams focused on student learning. Avoid operational conversations that can be communicated via email rather than taking precious paid collaborative time. Instead, stay continuously focused on the four critical questions to redirect discussions. They apply to all stages of the instructional cycle.

Team Members: Geometry teachers—Smith, Thomas, Hanson, Brown **Team Members Present:** Smith, Thomas, Hanson, Brown	**Date:** September 1

Planning Activities (Check all that apply.)	
Critical question 1: What is it we want our students to know and be able to do? ☐ Curriculum guides ☒ Pacing of power (or priority) standards ☐ Student-friendly learning targets ☒ Assessment design and planning ☐ Lesson plans ☐ Rubric design or scoring protocols Other:	**Minutes and Notes** • Review team norms. • Review essential standard document and determine additional examples of rigor needed for essential standard one. • Enter common formative assessment one and two into GradeCam (see https://gradecam.com). • Review state assessment data from last spring (last year's class).
Critical question 2: How will we know if each student has learned it? ☐ Common formative assessment data ☐ Student writing samples ☐ Student projects ☐ Rubrics ☒ Student results from district or state summative assessments ☐ Teachers' observation and anecdotal evidence Other:	**Curriculum Status Check (How is our pacing?)** On track
Critical question 3: How will we respond when some students do not learn it? ☐ Analysis protocols ☐ Daily, weekly, and long-term intervention planning ☐ Time built into the schedule ☐ Recovery plans ☐ Multiple ways to reassess Other:	
Critical question 4: How will we extend the learning for students who have demonstrated proficiency? ☐ Enrichment plans ☐ Extension plans ☐ Student choice ☐ Student leadership opportunities ☐ Community partnerships ☐ Celebrations and recognitions Other:	**Additional Support** • Hanson needs a new projector bulb. • Brown's classes are still not showing up in GradeCam.

Source: © 2020 by Fern Creek High School, Louisville, Kentucky; Nicolas, 2021, p. 154. Used with permission. Adapted from DuFour et al., 2016.

Figure 1.3: Team agenda template.

An efficient and effective master schedule allows you, as a leader, to ensure that instructional minutes are being met on each student, especially in elementary reading and mathematics or for high school credit requirements. It also allows you to provide teachers with non-negotiable collaborative time. Collaborative time during the day is essential for building an effective PLC culture and shared accountability. Common planning time by department rather than grade level ensures that the time is used to unpack learning standards, create common formative assessments, and plan for instruction and interventions. In the case of singletons, some schools choose to plan in grade levels or ranges of grade levels. This becomes more fluid but can still accomplish the focus of the four critical questions.

Have you ever thought about how important it is to have a plan for scheduling classes? It's kind of like putting together a giant puzzle. When we create a master schedule, we make sure that everyone is treated fairly, that we work together during a common team time, and that all students can learn at high levels.

This is especially important in high school, where we need to make sure that every student has an accurate schedule on the first day of school. But what about elementary schools? They often have classrooms where one teacher teaches all subjects or where teachers work together. In these cases, it might seem like a master schedule isn't as important. But even in elementary schools, we need to make sure that everyone is working together and that all students have the chance to learn and get the extra support they may need. This foundation will guide all instructional decisions made by campus leadership, coaches, interventionists, and teachers. Without a master schedule, you risk missing key opportunities to meet the needs of all students, fulfill required instructional minutes, and provide instruction in nontested content areas, like science. To get started, first identify the variables shown in figure 1.4.

Identify Schoolwide Times	Identify Extended Blocks	Identify Tier 2 Time	Identify Instructional Blocks	Break Down the Instructional Blocks
• Arrival • Breakfast • Morning meeting • Dismissal	• Lunch • Recess • Second recess • Specials and teacher planning	• Thirty minutes of reading • Thirty minutes of mathematics	• Reader's workshop • Writer's workshop • Mathematics workshop • Science and social studies • Other language components	• Mini-lesson • Explicit modeling • Closing and sharing

Source: © 2020 by Claire Springer. Used with permission.
Figure 1.4: Variables for master scheduling.

Being intentional with the scheduling of the school day helps support successful collaborative teams, which leads to improved student outcomes. Therefore, there are a few key items to note when looking at the difference between the logistics of scheduling for elementary and secondary schools. In the elementary setting, a single teacher typically has their students for the majority, if not all, of the day, with the exception of *specials* like physical education, art, and music. That means principals should mandate a schedule that includes state requirements for content area minutes (for example, ninety minutes per day for reading and sixty minutes per day for mathematics). As evaluators, principals should also know when science and social studies are taught. For example, during an observation, a principal should know what subject they are going to observe when entering the classroom on a given date and time according to the master schedule.

The elementary master schedule allows for creativity with intervention time. Schools often give intervention time an inspiring name, like *WIN* (what I need) time or a name including the school's mascot, for example. We don't want students to feel like needing extra support is punitive or shameful. To help alleviate this, principals can include other clubs and fun activities in the rotation, such as one intervention period biweekly for a club like yoga or robotics. You can also include social-emotional learning and team-building activities during this time. In elementary schedules, there is also the opportunity to swap groups of students so that they have the opportunity to learn from other teachers—ideally, the teacher with the highest achievement data for each learning standard or group of learning targets is able to take the students for intervention time in that standard. When you have at least two teachers at each grade level, this can be a fun practice to increase student engagement with a variety of educator perspectives and voices. As a reading teacher, I had intervention time on Fridays for forty-five minutes. We preplanned based on our data (three reading teachers were on my team), and each of us took a group of students who needed additional support based on the mastery of the learning targets for the week's lessons. We mixed all the students based on where they needed support to get to mastery, and we taught what our data indicated *we, as teachers*, were each strongest in that week.

Typically, teacher collaborative time in elementary school schedules can take place when students all go to specials. Intervention time is scheduled within the regular content area minutes for any of the core areas. This can be designated by the school's overall data. For example, if the school's SMART goal is that every student will be reading at grade-level proficiency by the end of the year, then intervention time may mean that all teachers and all support staff read with students for thirty minutes during an agreed-on time of the day. This is often a *drop everything and read* theme schoolwide. Figure 1.5 (page 14) shows an example of a master schedule from an elementary school.

14 | The Principal's Handbook for Priority Schools in a PLC at Work®

	Kindergarten	Grade 1	Grade 2	Grade 3	Grade 4	Grade 5
9:00	WIN (9:00–9:30)		Specials (9:05–10:00)		Mathematics	English language arts
10:00		WIN (9:55–10:35)	English language arts	WIN (9:55–10:35)		
		Mathematics		Specials (10:35–11:30)	WIN (10:50–11:30)	Mathematics
11:00						
	Lunch and planning	Lunch (11:50–12:30)		English language arts	Lunch (11:30–12:10)	Specials (11:30–12:25)
12:00			Lunch (12:10–12:50)			
		English language arts	Mathematics	Lunch (12:50–1:30)		Lunch (12:30–1:10)
1:00					Specials (1:05–2:00)	
				Mathematics		
2:00			WIN (2:00–2:40)		English language arts	WIN (2:00–2:40)
		Specials (2:30–3:25)				
3:00	WIN (3:00–3:30)					

Source: © 2022 by Joyce Parham. Used with permission.
Figure 1.5: Sample elementary master schedule.

The secondary schedule can be more complex because students attend different content-area classes with different teachers. Some have courses that are *singletons*—only offered once a day (typically, this is for honors or advanced placement courses but can also be foreign languages or any other specialty course that is not taken by large numbers of students). Minutes required in many states for seat time credit acquisition also make it difficult to include collaborative and intervention time for teachers in the schedule. High school intervention time is usually shorter than in elementary school due to credit requirements. As a leader, there are some ways to squeeze in additional intervention time after school if you can collaborate with athletic coaches and extracurricular sponsors to create a workable plan. I have found that student-athletes appearing on the honor roll can have an amazing impact on overall school culture. As a high school principal in a priority school, I incorporated thirty minutes of mandatory small-group tutoring for all student-athletes, and I partnered with the local university for tutors so that athletic coaches were not expected to teach high-level mathematics, for example. Asking coaches and sponsors to tutor inevitably leads to a "study hall" atmosphere, which is not effective academic support by most learning standards. Figures 1.6 and 1.7 (pages 16–19) are just two examples of creative scheduling.

In a small high school setting (with an enrollment of around four hundred students and few teachers covering common content and grade levels), the master schedule does not allow for common collaborative time during the school day, but it does allow flex time to be used for strategic interventions. The collaboration time is added to the end of the school day or in the morning but still within the contractual minutes.

A master schedule protects instructional time for students by ensuring that elementary students get adequate minutes in focus areas like reading and mathematics while not neglecting science and social studies. Protected time for elementary or high school students means that if time is built into the scheduled workday and designated with contractual language, then it is paid time that the guiding coalition can structure around best practices to improve student outcomes—not free time for making copies or scheduling appointments. A master schedule and accompanying documents that clarify expectations (norms and agendas) will allow leaders to monitor the time.

Room Number	First Period	Second Period	Third Period	Fourth Period	Fifth Period	Sixth Period	Seventh Period
Mathematics							
T133	Algebra I	Algebra I	Prep Period	Algebra I	Algebra I	Algebra I	Algebra I
M223	Algebra I	Algebra I	Prep Period	Geometry	Geometry	Algebra I	Geometry
M224	Geometry	Geometry	Prep Period	Geometry	Geometry	Geometry	Geometry
P210	Honors Precalculus (Trigonometry)	Honors Precalculus (Trigonometry)	Prep Period	AP Calculus	Algebra III	Algebra II	Algebra II
AC114	Transitional Mathematics	Transitional Mathematics	Algebra III	Algebra III	Algebra III	Prep Period	Athletics
P211		Algebra II	Prep Period	Algebra II	Algebra II	Algebra II	Algebra II
Language Arts							
T128	English 9	English 9	English 9	English 10	Prep Period	English 10	English 10
T127	English 9	Honors English 9	Honors English 9	English 9	Prep Period	English 9	English 9
MC203	Honors English 10	Honors English 10	Journalism	Journalism	Prep Period	Journalism	Journalism
P212	English 11	English 11	AP Language and Composition	AP Language and Composition	Prep Period	English 11	English 11
AC113	Transitional English	English 12	AP English Literature	English 12	Prep Period	AP English Literature	English 12
AC115	English 12	English 12	English 12	English 12	Prep Period	English 11	English 11
MC204	English 10	English 10	Critical Reading	Critical Reading	Prep Period	English 9	Critical Reading
P105	Personal Communication	Drama	Prep Period	Personal Communication	Personal Communication	Personal Communication	Personal Communication

Foreign Language						
M201	Spanish I	Spanish I	Spanish I	Spanish II	Prep Period	Spanish I
Science						
P101	Honors Physical Science	Honors Physical Science	Honors Chemistry	Honors Chemistry	Physical Science	Physical Science
M225	Biology	Biology	Biology	Biology	Biology	Biology
T120	Physical Science	AP Chemistry	Physical Science	Physical Science	Physical Science	Physical Science
P108	Honors Biology	Honors Biology	Biology	Biology	AP Biology	Physical Education
AC109	Environmental Science	Environmental Science	Chemistry	Chemistry	Chemistry	Chemistry

Source: © 2022 by Pine Bluff High Schools, Pine Bluff, Arkansas. Used with permission.
Figure 1.6: Sample secondary master schedule snapshot with common collaborative team time.

		First Period	Second Period	Third Period	Intervention Enrichment Flex Period	First Lunch	Fourth (A) Period	Second Lunch	Fourth (B) Period	Fifth Period	Sixth Period	Notes
English	A156	English 1–2	English 1–2	English 1–2	Flex		Prep			English 3–4	Honors English 1–2	
	A158	English 5–6	English 3–4	English 3–4	Flex		Prep			English 5–6	Honors English 3–4	
	A159	English 7–8	English 5–6	English 5–6 Honors	Flex		English 7–8			Prep	English 7–8	
Mathematics		First Period	Second Period	Third Period		First Lunch	Fourth (A) Period	Second Lunch		Fifth Period	Sixth Period	Notes
	A130	Prep	Algebra 1–2	Algebra 1–2	Flex					Math Lab 1–2	Algebra 1–2	
	A132	Algebra 1–2 Honors	Intermediate Algebra 3–4	Probability and Statistics	Flex		Algebra 3–4; 3–4 Honors			Prep		
	A129	Geometry 1–2	Geometry 1–2	Honors Geometry 1–2	Flex				Geometry 1–2	Intermediate Algebra 3–4	Prep	
	A137	Algebra 1–2	Applied Mathematics	Prep	Flex		Applied Mathematics			Applied Mathematics	Integrated Mathematics 1–2	
Science		First Period	Second Period	Third Period		First Lunch	Fourth (A) Period	Second Lunch	Fourth (B) Period	Fifth Period	Sixth Period	Notes
	A138	Biology 1–2	Honors Biology 1–2		Flex				Biology 1–2	Biology 1–2	Biology 1–2	
	A163	Physical Science	Prep	Software and App Design 3–4; 5–6	Flex		Business and Marketing 1–2			Business and Marketing 1–2	Software and App Design 1–2	
	A165	Earth Science	Prep	Environmental Science	Flex		Environmental Science			Chemistry 1–2	Earth Science	
	A163	Advanced Physical Education	Integrated Science	Alpha Student Success	Flex				Prep	Advanced Physical Education	Advanced Physical Education	
Social Studies		First Period	Second Period	Third Period		First Lunch	Fourth (A) Period	Second Lunch	Fourth (B) Period	Fifth Period	Sixth Period	Notes
	A127	Prep	Alpha Student Success	U.S. History	Flex		U.S. History			Alpha Student Success	U.S. History	
	A128	Prep	Government; Economics	Economics; Government	Flex				Alpha Student Success	Alpha Student Success (Mentor Group)	Government; Economics	
	A126	Prep	World History	World History	Flex				World History	Film Studies	World History	

	First Period	Second Period	Third Period		Fourth (A) Period	First Lunch	Fourth (A) Period	Second Lunch	Fourth (B) Period	Fifth Period	Sixth Period	Notes
Special Education												
A139	Study Skills	Co-teach	Study Skills	Flex					Prep	Study Skills	Study Skills	
A131	Study Skills	Study Skills	Prep	Flex					Study Skills	Study Skills	Co-Teach	
A171	Prep	Hybrid	Hybrid	Flex	Hybrid					Hybrid	Hybrid	
A154	Self-Contained	Self-Contained	Self-Contained	Flex	Self-Contained				Self-Contained	Self-Contained	Self-Contained	
World Languages												
A157	First Period	SecondPeriod	Third Period			First Lunch	Fourth (A) Period		Fourth (B) Period	Fifth Period	Sixth Period	Notes
	Spanish 1-2	Spanish 5-6	Yearbook	Flex					Spanish 1-2	Spanish 3-4	Prep	
Career and Technical Education												
A136	First Period	Second Period	Third Period				Fourth (A) Period	Second Lunch	Fourth (B) Period	Fifth Period	Sixth Period	Notes
	Video Production 1-2	Video Production 3-4	Law and Public Safety 1-2	Flex		First Lunch					Graphic Design 3-4	
B121									Graphic Design 1-2	Prep	Sports Medicine and Rehab 3-4	
A172	Physical Science	Prep	Software and App Design 3-4; 5-6	Flex			Business and Marketing 1-2			Sports Medicine and Rehab 1-2	Software and App Design 1-2	
Physical Education												
RM B116	First Period	Second Period	Third Period		Fourth (A) Period	First Lunch		Second Lunch	Fourth (B) Period	Fifth Period	Sixth Period	Notes
	Advanced Physical Education	Integrated Science	Alpha Student Success	Flex					Prep	Advanced Physical Education	Advanced Physical Education	
RM B123	Weight Training 1-2	Weight Training 1-2	Weight Training 1-2	Flex	Weight Training 1-2							
Fine Arts												
A145	First Period	Second Period	Third Period		Fourth (A) Period	First Lunch		Second Lunch	Fourth (B) Period	Fifth Period	Sixth Period	Notes
	Reading and Writing Lab	3-D Art	Drawing 1-2	Flex					Art 1-2	Prep	Art 1-2	

Source: © 2024 by Katy Strevell. Used with permission.

Figure 1.7: High school master schedule example with flex time for intervention.

Instructional Cycles

Collaborative teams in a PLC organize their work around cycles. The progression of the work is, therefore, predictable for the most part. This cycle repeats as teachers work through the pacing for their content for the year. Robert J. Marzano analyzed state standards and found that if teachers tried to teach all the standards for their content area at the same depth and breadth, students would be in school until the age of twenty-seven (Scherer, 2001)! That's why educators must discuss the content and review the agreed-on essential standards to be able to pace their courses, build in assessments, and share instructional strategies and reengagement solutions for interventions when students don't learn. The cycle repeats over and over. Figure 1.8 provides an overview of how a collaborative team engages in an instructional cycle.

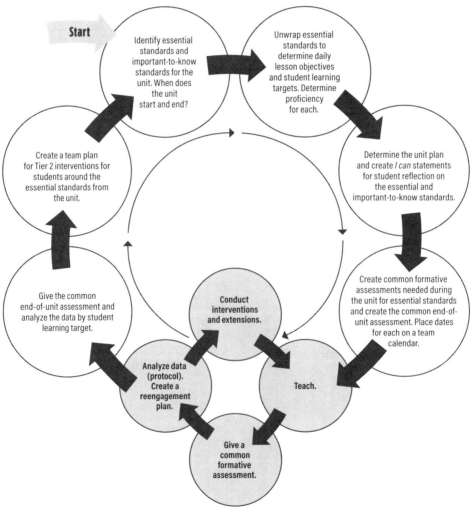

Source: Adapted from Kramer & Schuhl, 2017.

Figure 1.8: Summary of the work of collaborative teams in a PLC at Work.

Within instruction cycles, teams must consider several important variables, including the four critical questions of a PLC, the tiers of intervention (rigorous Tier 1 instruction, seamless small groupings for Tier 2, and intentional reinforcement in Tier 3), and the need to plan with the end in mind. Let's examine each of these in more detail.

Four Critical Questions

Teams with a PLC further break down cycles by leaning on four seemingly simple but critical questions (DuFour et al., 2024). On a unit-by-unit basis, collaborative teams answer the four critical questions with a focus on student learning (the first big idea of a PLC). Consider how your teams can gather and store their work for each unit so they can benefit from what they've learned in years to come. These questions guide the work of collaborative teams and help teachers develop a shared understanding of what students need to learn and how to support their learning. Principals should provide time and resources for teachers to collaborate around these questions. Following is a summary of the four critical questions and the work that collaborative teacher teams do with their guidance (DuFour et al., 2024).

1. **What do we expect students to know and be able to do?**

    ▸ *Look at the proficiency map for each unit*: Which standards are essential and *important to know*, and which standards are *nice to know*?

    ▸ *Unwrap any essential (or power) standard*: Be sure to determine student-friendly *I can* statements to use on team assessments and for data analysis and student reflection. Determine what it means for a student to be proficient with the standard.

    ▸ *Create a unit plan*: Use a calendar to map out the unit (consider typing this in a shared electronic doc to be used in the future). What are the daily learning objectives? When will the team give common formative assessments (for all or part of an essential standard)? When will the team give the end-of-unit common summative assessment, and which standards will it cover?

    ▸ *Ensure singleton teachers have a team*: Identify teachers (including singletons and special education teachers) who can work together on collaborative teams as they analyze student learning. What do students need to know and be able to do across the team? Teachers can collaborate on shared skills and look for shared content. A mathematics teacher can work with a physical education teacher to reiterate standards that are used in sports, such as statistics and geometrical figures found on basketball courts. In art, a teacher can explain perspective in drawings with geometry standards used to draw perspective, such as proximity or distance. A music teacher can teach the author's tone by asking students to watch a suspenseful car chase scene in a movie without the volume, and then the students write the music that appropriately conveys the tone intended by the suspenseful feeling they would like to convey. Create a proficiency scale or rubric to use across the team when assessing the skill in each subject area or grade level. The importance of discussing the learning standards and applying them across content areas can enrich a teacher's efficacy and reduce the isolation of a singleton in a small school. Teachers across content areas can also focus on commonly identified skills, such as writing to describe sequential phenomena: order of operations in culinary arts (recipe), science lab experiments that require chronological moves and measures, and career and technical courses that require reading and applying manuals for various career pathways. Teachers can help students make connections across content areas but also connect to the larger community outside of their school.

2. **How will we know if students learned it?**
   - *Create team common formative assessments*: These will be for each teacher to use during the unit for essential standards. The team will also generate a common end-of-unit assessment that includes essential standards. Include the *I can* statements on the assessments.
   - *Determine the team scoring agreements*: How many points is each question worth? How might students earn partial credit? Which rubric will the team use, if needed?
   - *Administer common assessments*: Teachers identify common timing on the calendar and agree on how it will be administered.
   - *Calibrate scoring*: Make sure each teacher scores student assessments consistently.
   - *Complete a data-analysis protocol with two areas of focus*: The data-analysis protocol should include (a) the number or percentage of students who are proficient, determining trends in student work, and a targeted plan for what to do during

Tier 1 or Tier 2 instruction, and (b) an analysis of which instructional practices were most effective.

- *Analyze common formative assessment to a target*: Each learning standard may have a few targets for students to learn. For example, for a student to understand characterization in a novel, the targets might be the following—I can identify physical attributes that help me visualize an author's character; I can identify how a character's thoughts as written by the author tell me about the character's personality and values; I can understand a character's behaviors through their words and actions as narrated by the author; and I can determine how developed or complex a character is based on the author's depth of characterization.

- *Analyze an end-of-unit assessment to multiple targets*: While formative assessment is a quick check to see if students understood the learning target (usually one to three targets), the end-of-unit assessment is the check of a larger unit, set of standards, and multiple targets.

3. **How will we respond when students do not learn?**

    - *Make a targeted plan for Tier 1*: This might include a mini-lesson, bell-ringers, station activities, differentiation, and so on, as needed, from common formative assessments.

    - *Make a targeted plan for Tier 2*: This would be instruction to an essential standard after the common end-of-unit assessment. Determine the plan as a team using a data-analysis protocol.

4. **How will we respond when students have learned?**

    - *Consider using some nice-to-know standards*: These would include those the team was not able to teach during the unit due to time limitations.

    - *Determine how to extend student learning*: Look for ways to deepen understanding of the essential standard other students are still working to learn.

While most schools traditionally go from Monday through Friday, some schools and districts pilot other schedules. For example, Monday through Thursday is the four-day week with enrichment or professional learning on Fridays. Other districts have early release for students one day a month for teacher collaboration time. Some schools are piloting Saturday school for a half day of intervention or enrichment time. Overall, this affects the instructional minutes in the day (four days of ten hours, for example) and the time teachers have to work through the instructional cycle. Generally, the cycle is two weeks. When teachers have more or less collaborative time, it can affect the depth and pacing with which they teach each standard, the creation and analysis of the common formative assessments, and the time to prepare for interventions. Therefore, though the cycle is loosely two weeks, it can also be measured or "chunked" by the unit. Traditionally, in a five-day school week, the instructional cycle can look like the example in figure 1.9. This can be an electronic document posted in a shared curriculum portal or folder that provides guidance and links to essential resources.

The teaching and learning cycle is about developing a guaranteed curriculum, which is often defined as a mechanism through which all students have an equal opportunity (time and access) to rigorous content, and a viable curriculum, for which there must be adequate time for both the teachers to teach the content and for students to learn the content.

Step 1	Step 2	Step 3
Review lagging data points.	Review academic standards.	Choose essential standards and create team SMART goals.
Student assessment portal ACT Aspire portal SMART data dashboard	State academic standards	Choosing essential standards in PowerPoint PreK–12 curriculum guides
Step 4	**Step 5**	**Step 6**
Create pacing guides and proficiency maps.	Unpack essential standards.	Plan formative assessments (add materials and resources).
PreK–12 proficiency maps PreK–12 pacing guides	Unwrapping the standards in PowerPoint Curriculum documents (K–12) A guide to writing effective learning targets Sample (elementary) Sample (secondary)	Assessment planning tool Sample of assessment planning tool
Step 7	**Step 8**	**Step 9**
Plan learning cycles by using the cycle guide to map out the number of days.	Plan daily direct, explicit lessons and engage learning activities by adding materials and resources.	Administer common formative assessments, analyze the data, and plan intervention and enrichment.
10-day learning cycle guide (Assess key: PLC) Elements of quality instruction	Daily lesson plans (templates only)	Data-analysis workbook Interventions and enrichment lesson plans (templates only) Sample data-analysis worksheet

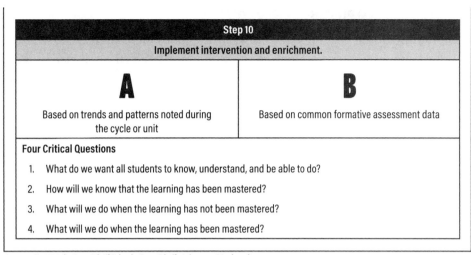

Source: © 2022 by Pine Bluff Schools, Pine Bluff, Arkansas. Used with permission.
Figure 1.9: The teaching and learning cycle.

Another example comes from *Charting the Course for Leaders* (Sanders, 2021; figure 1.10). This example strives to show the instructional cycle in another format: day by day for teachers to follow. In districts and states with numerous uncertified teachers, you may see the four critical questions depicted in a variety of ways to make them accessible to educators coming from a variety of backgrounds or pathways to the field of education.

The ten-day learning cycle is a plan for planning instruction, assessment, and intervention. The cycle is implemented only for essential standards.

Day	Task	Accomplished
1	Unpack essential standards. This process is ongoing.	[Revisit]
2	Create common formative assessments.	
3	Create a lesson plan using unpacked essential standards.	
4–7	Teach a lesson plan.	
8	Give a formative assessment and analyze those data; create an intervention lesson with differentiated instruction.	
9	From the intervention data, develop intervention groups.	
10	Reassess the *didn't get it yet* group.	

Source: Sanders, 2021, p. 226.
Figure 1.10: Ten-day learning cycle checklist.

*Visit **go.SolutionTree.com/priorityschools** for a free reproducible version of this figure.*

Tiered Instruction and Intervention

Schools and districts that operate as PLCs need a mechanism in place to respond to critical questions 3 and 4, which is most often done through tiered intervention, commonly known as response to intervention (RTI) or a multitiered system of supports (MTSS). While variations in these frameworks abound, in all cases, instruction and interventions occur at three tiers.

Tier 1 instruction is grade-level instruction that *all* students receive, even if they also receive higher-tier interventions (Mattos et al., 2025; Springer, 2020). Think of this tier as a promise to every student that the adults in the building are committed to ensuring that every student has the opportunity to learn what has been identified as a Tier 1 essential curriculum utilizing district resources and state standards.

Tier 2 intervention and extension is extra time to master grade-level curriculum (Mattos et al., 2025; Springer, 2020). This is the "bonus hour" for our essential standards. Tier 2 time can be built into regularly scheduled courses, especially in elementary school. Students who need more time to master the essential standard in mathematics or reading receive interventions on a specific learning target with which they need more practice. In addition, this time can serve as an extension block for those students who showed mastery of the essential standard. Priority schools are often faced with growing numbers of students who fall into tiered interventions for longer periods of time and lack a structure for addressing interventions for large numbers instead of small groups or individual students. Putting such a system in place can seem daunting, but getting started is necessary before you can solve the problem. Understanding more about the structures means also understanding how to ensure these supports are incorporated into the school day. Mattos and his colleagues (2025) visualize this process as an inverted pyramid (figure 1.11). Some excellent resources can help teams understand both the systems and processes, as well as how timely supports will help them move students out of the need for those supports over time. The foremost of these are the books *Taking Action, Second Edition* (Mattos et al., 2025) and *The Big Book of Tools for RTI at Work* (Ferriter, Mattos, & Meyer, 2025).

Tier 3 intervention is a specialized intervention to fill foundational grade-level gaps in learning from previous years or an extension program (Mattos et al., 2025; Springer, 2020). In priority schools, the most intensive tier of support is bloated and also difficult to tackle without the help of the entire school team. It's simply a matter of logistics, and if you have twenty-eight students to every

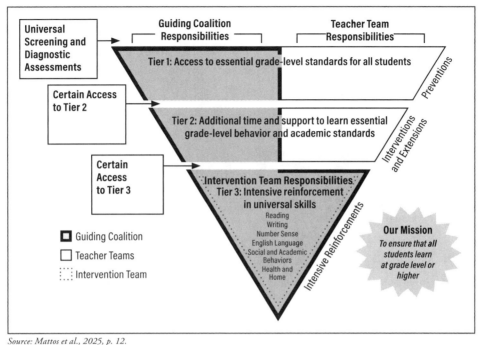

Source: Mattos et al., 2025, p. 12.
Figure 1.11: The RTI at Work pyramid.

teacher, intervening for five to six of them won't happen magically. In the most effective and efficient systems of support, every adult has students for some type of support or enrichment so that the best teachers for the students most in need can work in small groups. Even if Tier 3 is before or after school, at minimum, other adults are ensuring supervision so that students most in need get the support that is differentiated for them.

Backward Planning—With the End in Mind

In the realm of school leadership, effective planning is paramount to ensure the achievement of desired educational outcomes. One approach that has a lot of traction is backward planning (McTighe & Curtis, 2019; Wiggins & McTighe, 1998). This strategic method involves starting the planning process by envisioning the desired end and then working backward to determine the necessary steps and resources required to reach that goal. Although Grant Wiggins and Jay McTighe (1998) developed their theory to guide lesson and unit planning in curriculum, instruction, and assessment, the process applies to achieving goals or outcomes in systems planning. Researcher Brent Davies (2004) describes a *strategically focused school* as an organization where the systems are explicitly planned to lead to the results that a school leader has defined as the end outcome. In *Leading PLCs at Work Districtwide: From Boardroom to Classroom* (Eaker et al., 2021), the authors state that *moving from hoping to planning* entails tying every action to an ultimate goal: high levels of student learning for all. This means that a clear vision must be identified as the north star of the organization.

Benefits of Backward Planning

Backward planning offers several advantages to school leaders. By starting with the end in mind, leaders can develop a clear vision of their desired outcomes and align all subsequent actions accordingly. This approach promotes a strategic mindset, ensuring that every decision and resource allocation is purposeful and directly contributes to the end goal (Davies, 2004; McTighe & Curtis, 2019). Additionally, backward planning allows leaders to identify potential obstacles and challenges early on, enabling them to proactively address and mitigate these issues (McTighe & Curtis, 2019). As leaders, principals often encounter inherited systems that don't best serve students. One example is a system that only allows teachers to recommend students for honors or advanced courses. Some systems or processes are exclusionary and should be examined and discussed for needed updates.

Research Supporting Backward Planning

Organizational and educational studies have examined the effectiveness of backward planning to track steps to successfully achieve an individual or team goal. One notable study by Wiggins and McTighe (1998) demonstrates that educators who employed backward planning reported higher student engagement and achievement compared to those who used traditional planning methods. Clearly defining the desired outcomes and working backward to identify the necessary learning activities and assessments, teachers were able to create more meaningful and relevant instructional experiences for their students. This is the same strategy that can help leaders align every decision to the school's vision. Wiggins and McTighe (2005) continued to refine this model, looking not at all the content of a course first but at the intended outcomes and filling in the content needed to achieve mastery of the outcome in reverse fashion. James M. Lang (2010) and John Biggs (2003) articulate that the final learning outcome defines the activities, curriculum, and assessments that all come together to create a developed course using backward planning design.

According to Wiggins and McTighe (2005), backward planning design involves a three-stage process.

1. Identify desired results.
2. Determine acceptable evidence.
3. Plan learning activities.

This thought process starts with the end result and works backward, filling in all the steps on the journey to achieving the goal. Stephen R. Covey's (1989) enduring recommendation is to begin with the end in mind.

Elise Trumbull and Andrea Lash (2013) further examine the impact of backward planning on student performance and teacher instruction in a public school district. Their findings reveal that schools with leaders who embrace backward planning experience higher levels of student achievement across various content areas by supporting teachers through the process of designing with the end in mind and checking for understanding along the way using formative assessments. The researchers note that this approach fosters a culture of instructional coherence and provides a road map for teachers to follow, resulting in improved student outcomes (Trumbull & Lash, 2013). Davies (2004) finds the same concepts of backward planning presented by Wiggins and McTighe (1998) could be used by school leaders to aspire to a goal and plan backward for strategic progression to achieve the desired results.

In collaborative teams, we coach teachers to use pacing guides and curriculum standards to help start with the four critical questions and backward plan with the desired answers as their goals. School leaders can lead their departments through exercises using the backward planning process. For example, if the goal of the attendance clerk and counselors is to increase student attendance, the team would create a goal of 95 percent attendance in all mathematics classes for all students. Working backward from the goal, they will identify barriers to the goal and bring solutions to the table that they can implement. Perhaps the district transportation system is unreliable due to increased traffic within the school boundaries. An idea might be not to schedule mathematics as the first period. The team could pull attendance from all first-period mathematics classes and the correlating grades for students who are routinely missing the first part of class due to bussing, which is out of their control. This one action could have long-lasting positive outcomes for both learning and attendance data.

As another example, if the guiding coalition is seeking to increase relationship development with families but has tried evening and weekend events without success, perhaps transportation and caring for younger siblings prevent family members from packing up after work and heading to school. A principal could support an event at the community center of an apartment complex where many families live. By identifying goals with various teams and thinking outside of the status quo systems and procedures, a leader can help a team get results and support innovation.

Leaders in priority schools can do the same with their guiding coalition and other staff by identifying ongoing problems or barriers, either operational or academic, stating what the goal is, and then identifying the steps needed to reach the goal. Using discipline referrals as an example, an assistant principal and the counseling team might set a goal of eliminating behavior infractions in the hallway during passing intervals. To reach that goal, they may implement a reward system, dedicate time to positive behavior lessons at the beginning of each day, and commit to three positive phone calls to parents and guardians every afternoon. Setting benchmarks and reconvening to see if the actions are producing the desired effects is an ongoing cycle in the process of improvement.

Implementing Backward Planning in Public School Leadership

To effectively implement backward planning in school leadership, leaders can follow a systematic process.

1. **Identify the desired outcomes:** Begin by clearly defining the ultimate goals and objectives of the educational institution. This includes considering both academic and nonacademic outcomes, such as student engagement, social-emotional development, and community involvement.

2. **Determine the necessary evidence:** Identify the indicators or measures that will provide evidence of success in achieving the desired outcomes. This may include standardized test scores, graduation rates, student surveys, or other data sources.

3. **Design the assessment and instructional activities:** Working backward from the desired outcomes and evidence, develop a comprehensive plan that outlines the specific assessments and instructional activities required to achieve the desired results. This includes considering the curriculum, teaching strategies, resources, and professional development needs.

4. **Allocate resources:** Identify the necessary resources, including budgetary allocations, staffing requirements, and professional learning opportunities needed to support the implementation of the backward planning process.
5. **Monitor and adjust:** Continuously monitor progress toward the desired outcomes and make adjustments as necessary. Regularly collect and analyze data to inform decision making and ensure alignment with the overall goals.

Backward planning represents a powerful approach for school leaders to strategically plan with the end in mind. By clearly defining the desired outcomes and working backward to determine the necessary steps and resources, leaders can create a purposeful learning environment. Eaker and his coauthors (2021) state, "Effective leaders ensure a constant connection to the why: why each goal is particularly important, and how the goal contributes to the district's [or school's] mission of high levels of learning for all students, as well as the district's vision of the future" (p. 29).

Data Protocols

Monitoring collaborative teams also involves collecting and analyzing data on student learning and teacher collaboration. Teachers should use these data to identify areas of strength and weakness in student learning and provide targeted support and intervention for students to reach mastery of learning targets. Principals, in turn, can use the data to identify areas of strength to highlight for new or struggling teachers and provide targeted support and professional development for teachers and supporting staff. Implementing and monitoring collaborative teams requires a clear purpose, time, and resources; a culture of trust and respect; and a focus on student learning. Priority school principals can support a PLC at Work culture by following the framework outlined in *Learning by Doing* (DuFour et al., 2024).

Standardizing a data protocol will help eliminate the subjectivity about how teachers feel individual students are mastering content. The sample data protocol from Kramer and Schuhl (2017; figure 1.12, page 32) illustrates how a standard approach to data collection and correlating questions can help a team understand which students have reached proficiency, which students are near mastery, and which students need additional Tier 2 or 3 intervention time.

Data-Analysis Protocol

1. Determine the percentage of students proficient on the assessment for each standard or target by teacher and then for all students within the team. Write the information in the following chart.

	Target 1	Target 2	Target 3	Target 4
Teacher A	28%	13%	34%	22%
Teacher B	52%	29%	30%	21%
Teacher C	22%	21%	26%	14%
Teacher D	26%	33%	31%	32%
Total Team	32%	24%	30%	22%

2. For each standard or target, determine the number of students who are proficient, close to proficient, and far from proficient by teacher and as a team (write the number or the names of the students).

Target 1

	Proficient	Close to Proficient	Far From Proficient	Total
Teacher A	8 students	11 students	9 students	28
Teacher B	15 students	7 students	6 students	28
Teacher C	6 students	13 students	9 students	28
Teacher D	7 students	10 students	11 students	28
Total Team	36 students	41 students	35 students	112

Target 2

	Proficient	Close to Proficient	Far From Proficient	Total
Teacher A				
Teacher B				
Teacher C				
Teacher D				
Total Team				

Target 3

	Proficient	Close to Proficient	Far From Proficient	Total
Teacher A				
Teacher B				
Teacher C				
Teacher D				
Total Team				

Target 4

	Proficient	Close to Proficient	Far From Proficient	Total
Teacher A				
Teacher B				
Teacher C				
Teacher D				
Total Team				

3. What skills did the proficient students demonstrate in their work that set their work apart? Which instructional strategies did teachers use that effectively produced those results?

   The proficient students were able to give examples and show their work. Teacher B used rotating centers for targets 1 and 3, giving students multiple exposures to the methods she modeled in the explicit lessons. Students watched, practiced with a partner, and then practiced independently before moving through centers with various manipulatives. Students were able to group magnets to show their understanding of part-to-whole fractions, and this will scaffold to percentages with conceptual understanding.

4. In which area or areas did my students struggle? In which areas did our team's students struggle? What is the cause? How will we respond? Which strategies will we try next?

   My (teacher C) students struggled to understand groupings when I gave direct instruction on part-to-whole. Fewer were confident with the understanding and seemed to guess more. I didn't use manipulatives, and I think that would help with the hand-to-brain connection.

5. Which students need additional time and support to learn the standards or targets? What is our plan?

   We organized small group centers using Teacher B's plan with manipulatives in Tier 2 instruction in the instructional period. Students who are close to proficient and far from proficient will be in groups, with those who are far from proficient having reengagement with the original lesson in a small group with support from a paraprofessional. We hope to get all of the students closer to proficiency. If Tier 3 is needed, we will have students in the flex time as twenty-minute, one-on-one slots for the next two days.

6. Which students need extension and enrichment? What is our plan?

   Students who are proficient will work together to show their mastery in order formats and get creative. Our media specialist will help us try this.

7. Do these data show we are on track to meet our SMART goal? Why or why not?

   We are headed in the right direction to move all students to proficiency—our close to proficiency groups are growing. Once we have implemented the small groups and tiers, we will reassess and report results.

Source: Adapted from Kramer & Schuhl, 2017.
Figure 1.12: Data-analysis protocol.

*Visit **go.SolutionTree.com/priorityschools** for a free reproducible version of this figure.*

Reflection and Continuous Improvement

On the journey to continuous improvement in a priority school, celebrations for both students and staff are critical. Once the year is started, it is more difficult to plan reflectively and intentionally for celebrations. I suggest organizing a committee for student celebrations and a guiding coalition for staff celebrations so that both groups are recognized regularly. Friendly competition between grade levels and teams can create momentum and a fun sense of challenge to produce growth in student learning and help teachers keep their focus and creativity when they may be less motivated (before holiday breaks and spring assessments, particularly). Engage your parent-teacher organization (PTO) or student government to help. Being reflective before the year begins is important, but sometimes great ideas come randomly throughout or at the end of the year. Write them down. Take them to the team or committee for feedback. *You won't remember them—write them down!* A principal's reflection might look like this:

> November 20, 2023
>
> Today was an especially hard day. I had all my classroom observations planned, and a parent showed up unannounced; normally, my administrative assistant would have intercepted her and asked to set an appointment or at least had her wait in the lobby. I just happened to be walking by the front doors when she arrived, and although I tried to explain my observations and deadline, she raised her voice and threatened to call the district office and post on social media about how awful my school is. I tried to take a deep breath, but my frustration was all over my face. So, of course, I escorted her into my office. I saw an opportunity to get us some water, went to the refrigerator, and paused. I just needed to gather my thoughts and remind myself that she was angry, maybe scared, and most likely heard a different version of her child's horseplay that got him into trouble. I knew I should've called her earlier, but I had hoped it could wait. Nope. She immediately responded and took a side. I took a few deep breaths and went back to the office. I offered her the cold water and we both took a sip. "I'm glad you're here to discuss what happened in the classroom this morning," I said. "From what I was told by both your child and the other student, they were moving through an activity that had some beach balls to learn vocabulary, and it became a competition to throw it harder—just between some of the students. No one was hurt, and I think the conversation with your child was very productive." I could visibly see her deflate and let her guard down a bit. We had a much more positive conversation than I thought we were going to have. All in all, I was twenty minutes late for my observation, but I was able to get back on track within a couple of hours. Going forward, maybe some common ground can be found if I try to deescalate a conversation before we start a discussion.
>
> Then, the fire alarm went off, and it was not a drill! Thankfully, it was a prank and not a fire, but I scheduled a grade-level meeting with the sixth-grade teachers for tomorrow morning. This gives me a little time to review the cameras in the sixth-grade hallway. Since this is a pattern, I think we need to incorporate some morning meetings so I can set the tone for the day. I'm pretty sure someone will help me identify who pulled the fire alarm by the end of the day. I've been thinking about morning meetings for a while and the leadership team is on board. The teachers are thrilled.

Share the reflection habit with your staff. This can be introduced with a small journal with your school logo at the beginning of the year or on preservice days. Use it at the end of those days and ask teachers to reflect on their learning and what their hopes and goals are for the first days of school. The staff reflection tool in figure 1.13 is also helpful for this.

Staff Reflection Tool

As educators and professionals working in a public school, it is essential for us to continuously reflect on our practice and strive for personal growth. To facilitate this process, we have developed a Personal Reflection Tool, designed to help teachers and staff critically assess their performance, identify areas for improvement, and celebrate successes. This tool aims to foster a culture of self-reflection and professional development within our school community. By engaging in regular self-reflection, we can enhance our teaching effectiveness, ensure student success, and contribute to the overall growth of our educational institution.

Instructions:

1. **Set aside dedicated time:** Carve out a specific time each week to engage in personal reflection. This could be during planning periods, before or after school, or any other suitable time that allows for uninterrupted focus.

2. **Create a conducive environment:** Find a quiet and comfortable space where you can reflect without distractions. Ensure that you have access to any necessary materials, such as student data, lesson plans, or professional development resources.

3. **Reflect on teaching practices:** Consider your lessons, instructional strategies, and assessment methods. Ask yourself questions like the following.

   ▸ Did my lessons effectively engage students and promote active learning?
   _____
   _____

   ▸ Did I differentiate instruction to meet the diverse needs of my students?
   _____
   _____

   ▸ Did I provide timely and constructive feedback to facilitate student growth?
   _____
   _____

   ▸ Did I create a positive and inclusive classroom environment that fosters student success?
   _____
   _____

4. **Assess student progress:** Reflect on the academic, social, and emotional growth of your students. Evaluate the effectiveness of your instructional practices by considering the following:

   ▸ Did my students make progress toward their learning goals?
   _____
   _____

   ▸ Did I utilize formative assessments to inform my instruction?
   _____
   _____

   ▸ Did I address any barriers to learning that my students faced?
   _____
   _____

Figure 1.13: Reflection tool for all staff.

continued →

5. **Identify areas for improvement:** Based on your reflections, identify specific areas where you can enhance your practice. Set achievable goals that align with the school's mission and instructional priorities. These goals should be measurable, time-bound, and relevant to your professional growth.

6. **Seek feedback:** Engage in time to think about your progress and development. Plan goals with your team or supervisor to create actionable and timely benchmarks to mark growth.

Goal Area	Question 1	Question 2	Question 3	Question 4

*Visit **go.SolutionTree.com/priorityschools** for a free reproducible version of this figure.*

Conclusion

When it comes to leading a PLC in a priority school, the time we take to plan and reflect is critical to improvement, both as professionals and as an organization. Planning for conversations, meetings, celebrations, instruction, interventions, goal setting, and brainstorming is necessary to give us a break from the reactionary nature of the work and from some of the physically and emotionally exhausting days we inevitably encounter while working in schools at every level. A shared focus on something as simple as journaling can even be extended to students. How cool would an announcement be that asked everyone to stop and take three minutes to journal about what is on their mind—a personal accomplishment from the day or week? I've never heard it happen at any school I have visited, but it would make an impression! A reflective look in the rearview mirror and then a look at what opportunities lie ahead so we can plan as a team is also a great agenda item for teams.

While the PLC foundation I present in chapter 1 covers a lot of ground—norms, a collaborative culture, instructional cycles, data protocols, and continuous improvement—it's a critical springboard to the rest of this book. Bookmark this chapter and turn back to it as necessary as you progress, and don't forget that every school has to start somewhere. Implementing a PLC in a priority school is *always* a process of continuous improvement.

Chapter 2

Positive Work Culture

All stakeholders in an organization are change agents (Fullan, 1982, 1993). Teachers, administrators, students, and parents can be positive, negative, or neutral forces—all affecting the attempted change. Given this reality, creating momentum is one of the most impactful ways that a leader in a struggling school can start to address the status quo. It must involve visible changes that are noticeable to students, parents, and staff.

When you go into a school that is not taken care of, you are likely to quickly see visible indicators of lack of pride and inattention to detail. Addressing indicators like these is a low-stakes way to get a quick win and start the momentum of change: Start a trash pick-up challenge, provide free recycling receptacles, beautify the grounds, ask for parents to assemble and help with small classroom upgrades like cubbies or coat hangers, or challenge grade levels or hallway classrooms to be a part of a theme that can create competition around positive physical changes. Increasing the care of your surroundings can change the internal environment by establishing a compassionate climate and increasing readiness to learn. One idea that worked in a rural community of an elementary school included enlisting family members to help support landscaping on the school grounds, small maintenance projects, and upkeep of the school's common areas and athletic fields as a volunteer campaign. Strong relationships with families and caregivers can lead to opportunities for school events: Who owns a food truck? Who owns a landscaping company? Who coaches club sports?

Take the time to frontload relationships: Most people want an opportunity to be heard, and listening is a fundamental way to understand the context that you are inheriting as a leader. Knowing how your staff members perceive the school, leadership, parental support, and student capabilities as learners will exponentially pay dividends as the year progresses. What I have experienced in priority schools is that most of the staff do not have their own children attending the school. They live in another part of town to avoid having parent conferences at the grocery store. A telling sign that your school is on the road to improvement is when teachers bring their own children back to your school or use open enrollment to have them attend the school. Understanding the individual concerns and strengths of your team will help you know who to ask for help and when, how to offer support strategically, and which voices to amplify on your leadership team or guiding coalition.

Complainers are notoriously loud; whether through official channels or the "grapevine," they will be heard. The people in your organization who are willing to pitch in and help are usually not those who publicly toot their own horn. In my experience, it is mostly the complainers who are the loudest, so it is important to continuously share the things that your quietest people are doing to advance the work of improvement. In every school—even an F school by state report cards—there are superstar teachers who are doing whatever it takes for their students. Just ask the students; they will tell you who those people are. Culture needs continual attention to remain positive. As discussed in chapter 1 (page 5), plan for both collaboration and culture building with scheduled opportunities to build trust, gain feedback, and adjust. Refreshing the work of a school's committees can be an innovative way to update celebrations, bring families into the community, and grow transparency.

In my experience, what differentiates a priority school from other schools is a systemic lowering of expectations that, somewhere along the line, became the accepted status quo. The challenges become systemic, and not only do teachers have lower expectations of their students, but they often lower expectations of the support they expect from the district office and the wider school community. Understanding the historical context of your school community is essential to navigating change in priority schools. A common conversation I have in introductory meetings is trying to unravel the problem of the majority of students performing below grade level and how time doesn't allow for the number of students needing intensive intervention to be helped throughout the traditional school day if one is going to teach the grade-level curriculum tested by the state. I remember asking myself, "Where in the world do I start when so many things are broken in this system?"

Ultimately, this question can only be addressed by starting with the end in mind, which is the linchpin of the PLC process (Eaker et al., 2021). As established in chapter 1 (page 5), priority school principals can apply background planning to achieve systemic change in their schools (Davies, 2004; McTighe & Curtis, 2019). To successfully implement change, leaders should be aware of the change process as described by educational theorist and researcher Michael Fullan (1982, 1993), the type of educators they should expect to work with, their working relationships with key personnel, and role clarity.

The Change Process

At the beginning of the change process, there must be a moral driving force, led by the instructional leader, to seek improvement, keep a skeptical stance, and welcome innovation and discussion (Fullan, 1982, 1993). The school's culture is made up of the actions and words of all teachers, administrators, students, and parents; their interactions can become more positive and respectful instead of escalating and accusatory. It is my belief that through systematic organizational training and positive motivation, all stakeholders can work together as change agents. Change begins with each individual, but the team is the *we* that will make that change last and be sustainable. Teams may comprise individuals with different roles in the school community—teachers, instructional coaches, student peer mentors, leaders, counselors, and sometimes parents—but they have one goal in common: to increase student learning (DuFour et al., 2024). Even an A school fails some students if its success doesn't account for 100 percent of the students.

Anthony Muhammad and Luis F. Cruz (2019) discuss the importance of trust in creating a collaborative environment where leaders build credibility with teachers and the greater school community because they're open to being lifelong learners and create the expectation that we all get better by learning together. This means leaders are participants in action research and the cycle of teaching and learning. Fullan's (1982, 1993) research focuses on ways to create a school that is nurturing to *all* students and thus increases our students' academic, emotional, and social growth. This is hard, time-consuming work, but culture inevitably supports structures (Muhammad, 2018). One of the most fulfilling team experiences at my school occurred when we invited students to present their common formative assessment data to the academic leadership team, discussed what worked for them as learners, and gave feedback on what wasn't effective for their learning styles so we could improve our practices. Then, we invited families to hear their children speak about their learning growth. This process was very powerful and validated the work of the teachers.

According to educational researcher Anthony Muhammad (2018), a non-healthy (toxic) culture is not an impossible challenge to overcome. The school culture is summed up by the school's history, the teachers' experiences, and the community's perception of the school. A transformational leader must work diligently and methodically to improve the school environment daily. Cultural change is a vague and difficult idea to plan for. A reflective leader must observe and then take steps to ensure that all students are learning and that academic success is the main goal of the school (Muhammad, 2018). In my experience, this process can take from two to three years, depending on strategic planning in the first year and the context you are inheriting as a new leader. For example, if your predecessor was in the role for a long time, you may have to spend more time building trust. The change you want to see may need to happen slowly to help teachers and staff adapt. Including them in the long-term planning can help generate support. In a priority school, a leader has to focus more on building capacity because the teachers and staff need more professional development and feedback on classroom instruction, and that can be time consuming and emotionally taxing. Reflecting on my journey in school improvement, the stages of change (Fullan, 1982, 1993) looked like this.

1. **Initiation:** Building a foundation for change

    ▸ *Understand the context*—Who are your stakeholders, and what has their experience been? Their insights are important to your success.

    ▸ *Assess the emotional and cultural state of the school*—This includes morale, trust levels, and existing practices. Gather information through conversations, observations, and data analysis.

2. **Support:** Clarifying the purpose for the new way

    ▸ *Articulate the why*—Make sure stakeholders know what's behind the need for change to ensure it aligns with the school's mission and goals, especially if you are revisiting and revising those with the staff.

- *Engage stakeholders*—Identify key stakeholders (staff, students, family members, and guiding coalition) and involve them early to understand their perspectives.

3. **Trust:** Establishing credibility and relationships

    - *Be present and visible*—Spend time in classrooms, common areas, and events to connect with staff, students, and parents.

    - *Demonstrate empathy*—Actively listen to concerns and show understanding of the challenges people are facing.

    - *Follow through*—Take small, meaningful actions based on feedback to build trust and show you're committed to improvement.

4. **Transparent and ongoing communication:** Aligning everyone around the vision

    - *Communicate the vision*—Share your goals and intentions clearly, explaining how changes will benefit the entire school community.

    - *Establish open channels*—Create regular opportunities for communication, such as weekly updates, one-on-one meetings, or Q&A sessions with staff and families.

    - *Be honest and realistic*—Acknowledge the challenges and be transparent about what can realistically be achieved in the short term.

5. **Leadership capacity:** Empowering others

    - *Engage the guiding coalition*—Involve them in decision making and action planning to foster shared ownership of change.

    - *Empower staff*—Provide professional development opportunities aligned with school goals. Encourage teachers to lead initiatives or share expertise with peers.

    - *Promote collaboration*—Create structures (for example, committees or feedback loops for the collaborative teams that are so critical to a culture focused on the professional learning community pillars) where staff can work together to address challenges and support change.

6. **Quick wins:** Demonstrating early success
   - *Identify low-hanging fruit*—Address small but meaningful issues that can show immediate progress (for example, behavior management strategies or communication improvements).
   - *Celebrate successes*—Publicly recognize achievements, whether from staff, students, or parents, to build momentum and positivity.

7. **Momentum:** Transitioning to long-term change
   - *Set clear goals*—Work collaboratively to establish measurable short- and long-term goals for school improvement.
   - *Monitor progress*—Regularly assess how changes are being implemented and adjust as needed.
   - *Foster continuous feedback*—Keep communication open to gather ongoing input from all stakeholders.

8. **Sustained change:** Embedding practices into school culture
   - *Reinforce new norms*—Celebrate and model behaviors that align with the new culture.
   - *Evaluate impact*—Reflect on what's working and what isn't. Share results with stakeholders to maintain accountability.
   - *Plan for supporting capacity*—Ensure leadership capacity is built across the team so that positive changes are embedded and resilient to future transitions.

While there is no foolproof way to address change for every context, in my experience supporting leaders across the United States as they take on roles in priority schools, systematically addressing these steps means that leaders can manage change effectively. This ensures they are cultivating trust, fostering collaboration, and guiding the school toward sustainable improvement. It is important to see this plan as adaptable and be open to making revisions along the way.

In my journey as a new principal in a priority high school, I quickly realized that the status quo was deeply ingrained in the culture of the organization; I saw and heard this constantly through the words, habits, connotations, behaviors, and traditions that the school normalized. I leaned on the work of Anthony Muhammad and others to help me understand and navigate the change process with my teachers, staff, community, and students (Muhammad,

2018; Muhammad & Cruz, 2019; Muhammad & Hollie, 2011). Muhammad (2018) writes about the characteristics of highly effective schools and how these traits unify a school's staff to focus all efforts on the goal of increasing student achievement. According to Muhammad (2018), a school's culture plays a critical role in determining whether a school can address student challenges to achieve grade-level learning proficiency as prescribed by federal mandates and high-stakes testing.

Muhammad (2018) addresses the issue of educational equity highlighted by the No Child Left Behind legislation of 2001. The achievement gap between Black students and White students still exists, and according to Muhammad (2024), it will not be eradicated until educators acknowledge that the gap exists for many reasons, some of which are symptomatic of social systems that continue in education and throughout society. Jon Valant of the Brookings Institution notes the inherent problem with the term *achievement gap*, which sets the achievement of White students as the standard of measurement for all students (Sparks, 2020).

The 2023 average scores in reading and mathematics declined compared to 2020 for all student groups, as reported by the National Assessment of Educational Progress (NAEP), in many cases widening existing score gaps. For example, the 13-point score decrease among Black students compared to the 6-point decrease among White students resulted in a widening of the White-Black score gap from 35 points in 2020 to 42 points in 2023 (National Center for Education Statistics [NCES], 2023). See figure 2.1 (page 44) for a summarizing visual of these trends.

We can strategically offer supports by subgroup by using the data to group the students whose academic growth suffered the most in each content area. Students' growth at your particular school may or may not mirror these national trends, but it is critical to use your site data to create plans for *acceleration* (Kramer & Schuhl, 2017) because there is no way to reteach two years' worth of curriculum for the duration of school closures and online disengagement due to the pandemic.

Student achievement in priority schools can be affected by teen pregnancy, generational poverty, single-parent families, incarceration, and lack of health care. Muhammad (2024) asserts that having an education is a necessity to combat the many negative factors that our students face. Transforming schools is the best option that our society has to address the lack of support and the trauma after COVID-19 closures experienced by today's school-age students and educators.

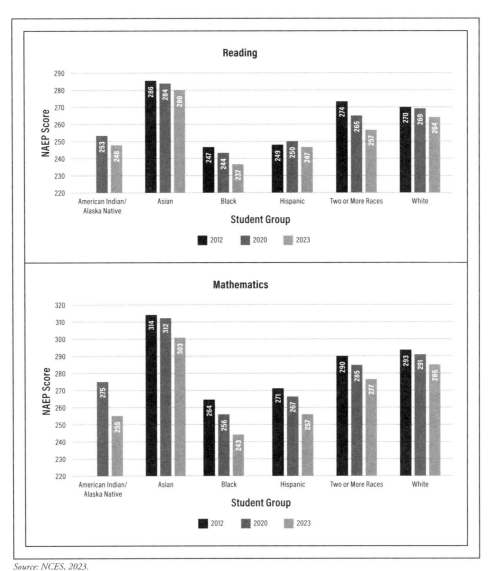

Source: NCES, 2023.

Figure 2.1: Changes in NAEP long-term trend reading and mathematics average scores for 13-year-old students by race and ethnicity—2012, 2020, and 2023.

Understanding and addressing the long-term impacts of the pandemic on learning loss, behavioral issues, social norms, and teacher recruitment programs continues to play out in schools without a lot of similar examples for educators to use as a blueprint. The New Teacher Project (2022) COVID-19 school response toolkit covers a variety of these big topics and provides templates for communication and ideas for improving communication, teacher morale, recruitment, retention, student behaviors, and learning with social-emotional supports and interventions. The New Teacher Project (2021) also offers a great resource called *Accelerate, Don't Remediate*, which I have used in my work in Arkansas and Arizona. The power and credibility of these documents lie at the crossroads of teacher-developed tools that are supported by research; The New Teacher Project takes their learning out of the theoretical into practical application in schools.

In his second book, *The Will to Lead, The Skill to Teach: Transforming Schools at Every Level*, Muhammad and coauthor Sharroky Hollie (2011) reiterate that there is a formula to improve chronically low-performing schools, and their goal is to help educational leaders implement their strategic formula to diagnose, treat, and eventually heal the underlying issues that plague ineffective schools. Muhammad and Hollie (2011) point out, "Despite statistics, student ethnicity and social class are not barriers to learning; rather, schools that do not properly respond to the needs of these students are the barriers" (p. 204).

Being able to quickly adapt as a learning organization is critical to implementing effective systematic change. The mindset shift starts with an acceptance that flexibility is more harmonious than rigidity; by opening up to asking "Why?" and considering how our structures serve students, a leader can model the open mindset that is necessary for positive change. The rest of this chapter addresses how staff members at any school fall into various groups and how leaders in priority schools can work with key stakeholders to ensure all groups are working together to promote school improvement and student achievement. Understanding the dynamics of how these educators behave and react to each other and students is especially critical when a leader is diagnosing the status quo and formulating a plan for systemic change.

Types of Educators

Muhammad (2018) asserts that school culture is the underlying determinant that will impact student achievement and the ability of educators to close the achievement gap among various student groups. The culture of a school may be toxic or healthy, or somewhere in between, and a transformational leader will need the tools to assess where a school lies along that spectrum, which directly relates to school effectiveness. Muhammad (2018) brings to light the different types of educators and how they influence student achievement and the culture of a school. The framework he provides seeks to guide a school leader in implementing the cultural changes that will maximize a school's effectiveness in improving student academic achievement and closing gaps among student groups. It poses that the underlying barriers to student academic success can be overcome by the purposeful and data-driven actions of educators when they believe that all students can learn.

Muhammad (2018) identifies the four different types of educators, as detailed in the following sections, who create the type of school culture that exists in all schools.

1. **The Believer:** Whose major goal is to provide academic success for each student
2. **The Tweener:** Whose goal is to strive for organizational stability
3. **The Survivor:** Whose goal is emotional and mental survival
4. **The Fundamentalist:** Whose goal is maintaining the status quo

The Believers

The Believers are teachers who have taught for three or more years; they are the "cheerleaders" of the school, who are student-centered and critical team members for transforming a school's culture (Muhammad, 2018). This group will be flexible and adapt to the needs of the students, focusing on student success, which drives all that they do. Believers are involved in the school community and will help the instructional leader create the type of school environment that is necessary to move from a toxic culture to an effective, positive culture that supports student success (Glanz, 2000). One consistent group that I have observed in every priority school I've been in remains the power of the Believers; during challenging times, their mindset is to acknowledge the barriers but move to solutions. Believers are not afraid to challenge policies that perpetuate classroom inequities and the status quo. They use positive actions and words to influence their peers and make student success the foremost goal in their classrooms. Believers are the risk-takers in the school, experimenting with technology, rewards, and collaborative methods to engage and motivate their students.

The Tweeners

The Tweeners are new teachers or those who try not to take sides with other groups (Muhammad, 2018). Tweeners believe in the school's mission and are trying to find their place in the school organization; for the instructional leader, this is a key group to bring onto the side of the Believers. The Tweeners can be persuaded to either support the students or just ride the fence. They are critical if a leader is seeking to transform the school's culture and adequately address student achievement.

Tweeners often have loose connections to the community; they may live outside of the school's boundaries, not seeing their students often outside the school environment. This causes a disconnect that must be intentionally remedied by building relationships with the students in the classroom and school through a variety of strategic activities, such as clubs, advisory periods, and athletics. Tweeners often feel an obligation to give back to society through their chosen profession of education; this characteristic can be used by the instructional leader to spur more ownership of students' success on the part of Tweeners. In my experience, Tweeners in a priority school are there to fulfill their own moral purpose.

The Survivors

Survivors are ineffective teachers who may be veterans or newer educators (Muhammad, 2018). They are just trying to make it to the end of each day, each week, and each school year. The Survivors are unmotivated to grow as professionals and do not seek any higher career goals in education. Survivors are often so stressed out and frustrated that they are unable and unwilling to see past their own situation to focus on student achievement. These are typically the most ineffective educators and can undermine the school's level of effectiveness overall. Often, Survivors are unable to manage various aspects of their own lives, making them incapable of managing the aspects of the classroom that are linked to a positive learning environment, such as behavior management, rituals and routines, and equitable student expectations. Survivors will keep the school culture in a state of stagnation, as these educators cannot plan and dream for the future vision of the school. Similar to the Fundamentalists, they are stuck in the status quo. In a priority school, I would say that Survivors will eventually leave the organization rather than change their mindset. They will actively work to subvert change that is difficult and must be addressed one-on-one by the leader.

The Fundamentalists

The last group, as labeled by Muhammad (2018), is the Fundamentalists. These individuals seek to maintain the status quo; they do not believe that all students can learn and are focused on those students who are self-motivated. Fundamentalists often reminisce about the "good old days" of education and blame external factors for the lack of success of some of their students, especially minority students (Muhammad, 2018; Peterson & Deal, 2002). This group tries to recruit the Tweeners into their camp, and the Believers and the instructional leader must be aware of the sabotaging effects that the Fundamentalists have on the school culture. Fundamentalists view change as the antithesis to success, making them dangerous opponents of transformational change. A leader seeking to improve school culture must continually use data and research to combat the efforts of Fundamentalists in their school. Fundamentalists often believe in the elitist assertions of the *bell curve* (Muhammad, 2018)—in other words, that a certain percentage of students are below average, average, and above average and that these roles depend on students' own capabilities and are unlikely to change. The bell curve has a fundamentally baked-in assumption that in any group, some learners will advance, and some will achieve below expectations, as a general rule. This deficiency mindset is antithetical to the belief that all students have the potential to learn at high levels. These educators tend to actively use tracking to categorize their students in terms of ability and intelligence.

Group Interactions

These four groups essentially make up the school's staff, and according to Muhammad (2018), an educational leader can better address each type of staff member by analyzing which group they fall into. Thus, leaders can understand their underlying motivations and how they influence the school's ability to address student needs and academic success. Muhammad (2018) asserts that time spent uncovering how these groups interact in a school will help a leader understand and strategize about how to bring about change in any particular school.

The priority school principal seeking transformational change must enlist the help of the Believers and Tweeners to combat the Fundamentalists' agenda of maintaining the status quo. Fundamentalists work through the informal "grapevine" of communication, using rumors and gossip to undermine positive changes in the school. Like the Survivors, the Fundamentalists resist change, but often for different reasons. The instructional leader is the key central figure in the people who make up a school's community; Muhammad (2018) dedicates part of an anthology to the all-important instructional leader, and the role that can change a failing school by uniting the staff in a positive culture for change (Eaker, DuFour, & DuFour, 2002; Maxfield, 2016; Muhammad, 2018).

Working Relationships With Key Personnel to Align Your Vision

In *Professional Learning Communities at Work: Best Practices for Enhancing Student Achievement* (DuFour & Eaker, 1998), the book that PLC educators and colleagues often say started a teaching and learning revolution, *interdependence* is the glue that holds an effective team together while allowing members to be fluid in responding to student needs. Muhammad (2018) states that teachers and administrators must be self-reflective, even when receiving positive job evaluations, and ask if *all* students are learning in their classroom and their school. This is directly connected to the school's culture and the belief that all students can and will learn due to the actions of teachers. The following three predetermining factors formulate a school's culture (Muhammad, 2018).

1. **Perceptual predetermination:** This is an educator's own socialization and the impact of that socialization on their practice in the classroom, including expectations for student performance. Our lived experiences as students are reflected in our expectations of the students we teach. Perceptions about students' capabilities, the organization's learning standards, and our efficacy as educators play out every day in classroom instruction. I have seen that aspirational perception change over time in a priority school setting because the work is challenging on a higher level every day.

2. **Intrinsic predetermination:** This is the student's perception of their probability of succeeding in school; these include messages a student receives from home, community, and school. One of the biggest achievements that I am proud of as a former priority school principal was the improvement in student confidence that came with higher achievement. When we believe we are capable of something, we are more apt to work until we achieve a goal.

3. **Institutional predetermination:** These are institutional barriers of policies and procedures ingrained within the walls of public schools that are the traditional way of getting things done. Inequities are a part of our nation's educational system. A Royal Society of Arts (2010) sketch art video visualizing the ideas of Sir Ken Robinson, an education and creativity expert, is a clear explanation of the historic predetermination of educational opportunities.

We can start to reshape the low perceptions and expectations that are pervasive in priority schools when we model language, behaviors, and results that indicate a higher level of excellence. Amazing things are happening in classrooms of priority schools all around the United States, but unfortunately, the bright spots are not always highlighted for the school community or are overshadowed by a negative reputation. We, as leaders, have an obligation to create better systems that showcase effective teachers and students whose excellence may be in the minority.

Meeting With Staff Members

In the dynamic education landscape, effective leadership in priority schools is crucial for fostering a positive, collaborative culture that supports an environment of growth and success. It's important for leaders, especially those new to the role, to schedule one-on-one face time with every employee. As a priority school principal, I found that meeting with each staff member, even for a brief fifteen to thirty minutes, helped me understand their mindset about student potential in the school. Even as a superintendent, I have a conference with each new employee (teachers, staff, administrators, and support personnel) to make a personal connection. There is no set agenda, but I find that the opportunity to ask questions such as "What's going well?," "What should we stop doing?," and "What should I know about you as an employee and community member?" are invaluable and a worthy use of that time. Through these observational and organic conversations, a picture of the true working culture emerges. Getting to know the teachers, their types and perspectives about education, as well as students and their concerns, will help any new principal have both celebratory and hard conversations that are valued and impactful. The leader could then bring to light the types of educators in the school and have conversations about their motivations and how to help get everyone working collaboratively and authentically.

Providing Role Clarity

Another key aspect of effective leadership is ensuring role clarity among all school personnel. *Role clarity* refers to the clear understanding of one's duties and responsibilities within an organization. When everyone knows exactly what's expected of them, they can do it. When people are unclear about what exactly their role encompasses, the burden falls on the principal. Being the central filter for all questions and concerns in a school organization is unsustainable for a principal. I've often discussed with priority school principals how exhausting the role is and how breakdowns in processes can appear if the principal is temporarily unavailable. The principal should not be the go-to person for all concerns that staff members can often handle at the source—for example, the registrar for enrollment, the assistant principal for discipline, or the media specialist for technology needs. One commonality that I observe in priority schools is a lack of procedures and systems that can be sustained without being filtered through the principal for all individual cases.

Ambiguity in roles also erodes trust because it sets us up for loose systems where tasks and events can fall through the cracks. This will inevitably lead to scenarios where people feel like they are scapegoats because they were not clear about what their roles were in the first place. In these cases, people, therefore, feel they are being held accountable without even knowing their responsibility for a particular task or event.

Understanding the scope of responsibility for each position in the organization fosters ownership. It serves as a foundation for effective communication, collaboration, and decision making in any professional setting, including schools. Effective communication sets the foundation for clarity of the interdependent nature of school guiding coalition roles. Sylvia Melena (2018) writes, "Listen more and talk less to gain a deeper understanding of each employee's needs, priorities, hopes, dreams, fears and concerns" (p. 27). Reciprocal and frequent communication builds trust and a common lens for the work at hand.

Numerous studies have highlighted the importance of role clarity in organizational settings. For instance, a study by Jeffrey Fermin (2022) finds that role clarity significantly influences job satisfaction and organizational commitment among employees. When employees clearly understand the expectations of their role, they are more likely to feel motivated to meet the standards set for them and less likely to experience burnout. In the context of schools, a study by Philip Hallinger and Ronald H. Heck (2010) reveals that role clarity among school leaders positively correlated with teacher job satisfaction and instructional improvement. These findings emphasize the need for school leaders to prioritize role clarity as a means of enhancing staff morale, job satisfaction, and overall school effectiveness.

Often, I have staff members whose work overlaps. For example, counselors and social workers might both reach out to offer support to parents, families, and students. Depending on the type of communication and support offered, this can lead to conflicting messages or inefficiency. Especially during preservice days, it can be useful to clarify roles for the teams within the school's departments. Ongoing weekly or biweekly meetings can continue throughout the year to ensure that responsibilities are interdependently supportive but not redundant.

By providing a detailed description of duties and responsibilities for each staff member, school leaders can foster an atmosphere of accountability, collaboration, and professional growth. In creating these roles, I advise adding the name or position to ensure that the team is aware of who holds the work or who to approach with questions or concerns. Figure 2.2 (page 52) shows how this role breakdown might look for a principal working together with middle school and high school assistant principals and an administrative intern.

Principal	High School Assistant Principal	Middle School Assistant Principal	Administrative Intern
(All Grades)	*(Eleventh and Twelfth Grades)*	*(Seventh and Eighth Grades)*	*(Ninth and Tenth Grades)*
Breakfast cafeteria duty daily After-school lobby duty	Breakfast duty, front lobby duty, and student parking lot duty	Breakfast duty, front lobby duty, and after-school bus duty	Scanner duty daily (morning); bus duty (afternoon)
Teacher evaluations as assigned	Teacher evaluations as assigned	Teacher evaluations as assigned	Discipline and interventions for ninth and tenth grades
Enterprise board meetings Finance academy board meetings	Meet with parent-teacher-student association		Supervise social studies collaborative team
Discipline and interventions for all grades as needed	Discipline and interventions for eleventh and twelfth grades	Discipline and interventions for seventh and eighth grades	Supervise after-school tutoring
Supervise high school athletic and fine arts activities as needed	Supervise high school athletic and fine arts activities as assigned	Supervise middle school athletic and fine arts activities as assigned	Supervise Saturday school and duties as assigned
Communicate with teachers, parents, and students regarding referrals, discipline, and grades	Communicate with teachers, parents, and students regarding referrals, discipline, and grades	Communicate with teachers, parents, and students regarding referrals, discipline, and grades	Communicate with teachers, parents, and students regarding referrals, discipline, and grades
Lunch duty as needed	Lunch duty (third lunch)	Lunch duty (first lunch)	Lunch duty (second lunch)
Student enrollment and individualized education plan (IEP) meetings as needed	Student enrollment and IEP conferences for eleventh and twelfth grades	Student enrollment and IEP conferences for seventh and eighth grades	Student enrollment and IEP meetings as needed for ninth and tenth grades
Attend suspension hearings (all grades) as needed	Attend suspension hearings (eleventh and twelfth grades)	Attend suspension hearings (seventh and eighth grades)	Attend suspension hearings (all grades) as needed
Testing coordinator supervision for committee and counselors	Assist with highly qualified reports for accreditation (high school)	Assist with highly qualified reports for accreditation (middle school)	Assist state highly qualified and accreditation reports for internship
Organize open house and parent conferences	Supervise high school testing with testing coordinator and high school counselor	Supervise middle school testing with testing coordinator and middle school counselor	Assist high school and middle school testing as stipulated by district and state requirements
Organize and lead faculty meetings and campus professional learning	Prepare testing data and upkeep of tracking documents	Help facilitate campus professional learning	Help facilitate campus professional learning

Organize and lead guiding coalition and campus improvement	Coordinate home language surveys (multilingual learners)	Coordinate and schedule extracurricular activities for middle school	Assume safety drills (with support)
Work with department chairs to ensure PLC fidelity; organize campus instructional leadership team meetings	Student information system data entry with high school counselor	Organize seventh-grade orientation	Observe content-area collaborative teams with administrative team (social studies)
Meet with department collaborative teams (English, academy as needed)	Meet with department collaborative teams (science and career and technical education)	Meet with middle school grade-level collaborative teams (mathematics and special education)	Participate in focus walks
Organize and participate in focus walks	Participate in focus walks	Participate in focus walks	Attend administrator meetings
Organize and attend administrator meetings	Attend administrator meetings	Attend administrator meetings	Supervise Saturday school
Monitor the student information system for weekly grade input	Monitor the student information system for weekly grade input	Monitor the student information system for weekly grade input	
Supervise Saturday school and after-school tutoring as needed	Testing lead	Supervise after-school tutoring as assigned	
Organize new teacher mentoring meetings	Facilitate safe schools committee	Facilitate Title I meeting for staff and parent nights	Other administrative duties as assigned
Create budgets for middle school and high school	Coordinate ACT fall and spring with testing coordinator and high school counselor	Evaluate support staff	Create and revise duty schedule as needed with faculty advisory committee leader
Coordinate concurrent enrollment	Oversee virtual learning students with high school counselor	Send out do-not-admit list daily	Order tests and facilitate testing administration professional learning
Coordinate calendar with financial secretary, athletics department, and fine arts department	Alternative education referrals (eleventh and twelfth grades)	Facilitate Title I meeting	Check certifications of new staff on state department of education website (to see if they need adjunct forms)
Evaluate support staff	Evaluate support staff	Support staff evaluations as assigned	Faculty advisory committee meetings
Support staff professional learning	School improvement plan coordinator (Title I plan)	Other administrative duties as assigned	
Set up testing meeting for all administrators, counselors, and teacher leaders	Advancement via Individual Determination (AVID) supervision	WAVE data entry with middle school counselor	

Figure 2.2: Division of roles and responsibilities.

continued →

Assign extra duties and coaching positions	Other administrative duties as assigned	Organize eighth-grade graduation ceremony	
In school academy such as academy of finance director	Maintain master schedule		
Evaluate administrators	Support staff evaluations as assigned		
Oversee building maintenance and operations			
Coordinate SATs with site test administrator			
Oversee 1:1 tech program with media specialist			
Conduct final review of high school and middle school accreditation reports			
Organize quarterly PLC data summits			

Role clarity forms the foundation for successful working teams. Using a tool to clarify roles and responsibilities helps team members understand the work lanes and when they intersect. The research supports the notion that role clarity positively impacts job satisfaction, organizational commitment, and instructional improvement. As such, prioritizing role clarity is essential for fostering a collaborative culture and effective learning environment within schools.

The assignment of roles and responsibilities for guiding coalitions should be equitable, and if you are lucky enough to hire your team members, you should look for complementary skills and abilities. This will allow you to assign teams based on the content area of your administrators and also to ensure that all get some experience with instructional leadership, as well as plant operations and organizational management.

A detailed description of duties and responsibilities for all school personnel, including teachers, teacher leaders, support staff, interventionists, administrative assistants, assistant principals, counselors, administrative interns, and school resource officers, will help school leaders empower their staff members to excel in their roles.

Teachers

Teachers are responsible for facilitating student learning and growth. A detailed description of duties and responsibilities for teachers should encompass areas such as planning in non-negotiable collaborative teams, delivering instruction, assessing student progress, and fostering a positive learning environment. Non-negotiable collaborative team time is part of the contractual day in many districts; therefore, the priority school leader can set parameters for that time to be used around the four questions that should be part of all the team agendas. In a PLC, this is referred to as a collaborative team meeting. When team time is after school or negotiable, it is often interpreted as optional, and when that occurs, some teachers will opt out, also opting their students out of the benefits of collaborative planning time. By being clear that collaborative team time is not optional, school leaders enable teachers to focus on their core responsibilities, leading to increased learning for all students. Principals can choose to incorporate that non-negotiable collaborative team time into their master schedules as long as other mandatory minutes are met (for example, some districts and states mandate ninety minutes of reading instruction daily), but there is generally site flexibility for a principal to incorporate non-negotiable time into the workday for teachers to collaborate.

Teacher Leaders

Understanding the mindsets of the teacher leaders is critical to getting everyone focused on student success. Although every teacher can be a leader, teacher leaders are often those who are designated to facilitate or coordinate grade-level or content-area collaborative teams. New principals should assess the capabilities and knowledge of inherited teacher leaders so that they're able to help drive the work of each team forward. Especially in priority schools, there is a sense of seniority that often drives the election of those leaders, and it may or may not be aligned with the direction of the future needs of the school as much as the maintenance of the status quo.

Every school has a culture that is shaped by what teachers believe about their own effectiveness—their collective efficacy—and students' potential. Some cultures are hospitable for adult and student learning; others are toxic. A school's culture can work for or against improvement and reform. The good news is that culture is mutable if a leader understands that people must be met where they are with a careful balance of acceptance, courage, motivation, and a proven system for improvement. The mindset of the teacher leader can often affect the entire team's capability to adapt to change, implement new procedures, or work with efficiency and shared accountability.

With the collaboration of the guiding coalition or leadership team, the principal can lead systematic change with the appropriate monitoring in place. Cultures sustain structures, according to Muhammad and Hollie (2011). They delve further into the study of types of educators and identify the two basic areas that a leader needs to assess and develop in educators: (1) willingness to be a change maker for students and (2) professional training and talent in engaging students in learning. According to them, educators must act on the belief that all students can learn and that our teaching must be shaped by the diverse needs of students rather than the convenience of the teachers (Muhammad & Hollie, 2011). Instructional leaders can lead transformation by combining the development of the learning environment with the development of instruction (Muhammad & Hollie, 2011).

The willingness of a culture rests in the staff's ability to adapt to the needs of the students and meet them where they are in their learning. The instructional leader must help educators set goals, overcome frustrations, set aside time for collaboration, and ensure that all activities are focused on decreasing student achievement gaps (Muhammad, 2018; Muhammad & Hollie, 2011). Teacher leaders can also help focus teams on valuing the identities, native languages, and cultures of students from marginalized backgrounds. They can encourage the instructional development of teachers, which is critical in giving them the tools they require to respond to diverse student needs.

Support Staff

Support staff members, including custodians, cafeteria workers, and bus drivers, contribute to the smooth and efficient functioning of a school. Clearly outlining their duties, such as maintaining cleanliness, preparing meals, or ensuring safe transportation, allows for efficient coordination and collaboration among all personnel. In some small schools or districts, support staff provide a broader range of support for families and students. In one district I observed, the new principal needed support in outlining the duties of the custodian. Classrooms and restrooms were not being cleaned daily, and when the principal was notified numerous times and could not locate the custodian, a daily meeting had to be set. Eventually, the meeting was moved to weekly. This is a quick win, as teachers saw immediate results. During COVID-19 closures, as a superintendent, I had the governing board's support to keep all staff employed by offering support in Zoom sessions, delivering meals to students and families, and providing devices and hotspots to students without home internet. These and other creative ways of supporting the community were outside of the scope of their job descriptions but allowed these employees to earn a paycheck to take care of their families.

Interventionists

Interventionists play a critical role in supporting students who require additional academic or behavioral assistance. A detailed job description may involve assessing student needs, planning interventions, and collaborating with teachers and parents. By clarifying the roles and responsibilities of interventionists, school leaders ensure that these professionals can effectively support students' individualized needs.

Administrative Assistants

The administrative assistant or office manager (the title may depend on state or district organization, but essentially function the same) plays a pivotal role in ensuring efficient administrative operations within a school. Responsibilities may include managing student records, coordinating communication with teachers and staff, and ordering supplies.

After years of experience, I've come to believe that the administrative assistant knows everything that happens in a school organization, and often, even within the neighboring community. The role is critical for an effective school: family members who are scared, angry, excited, or concerned often speak to the administrative assistant first. They are often the first ones parents see when they enter the school with anticipation to enroll, come in to meet a teacher or administrator in response to a voicemail, or arrive to check out a sick child from the nurse's office. They are the welcoming and compassionate face of the school, and it often falls to them to defuse emotional situations. This frontline person is critical to the school's reputation and perception among the greater community.

Teachers who are in turmoil, feeling enthusiastic, or have a personal emergency often tell the administrative assistant before the principal. They may let on their feelings about nondiscussables, an important aspect of school culture that might be difficult for especially new principals to unravel (Saphier & King, 1985). *Nondiscussables* are subjects of sufficient importance that are talked about frequently by the teachers and staff but are so laden with anxiety and fearfulness that these conversations take place only in places like the parking lot, the teachers' lounges, the playground, or the copy room. Fear abounds that open discussion of these incendiary issues—at a faculty meeting, for example—will cause a meltdown. The nondiscussable is the elephant in the room. Each school has its own nondiscussables, and the administrative assistant usually knows what these issues are—they are often a historical tradition inherited by each new leader.

Administrative assistants have true insight on the school's culture. They are often dynamic problem solvers, and principals should treat this relationship with care—they can often make or break other relationships for a new principal in a priority school. I maintain that the front office staff gets all sides of every story—from teachers, families, students, and other staff members. A morning check-in between the principal and administrative staff is a must. This sets the tone for the day and gives everyone a heads-up on anticipated issues. A weekly meeting of thirty minutes to an hour should be a standing calendar event. This helps ensure that everyone is knowledgeable about weekly school events, news, or procedural changes that affect families. A simple note-catcher like the example in figure 2.3 can help gather these disparate items.

Administrative assistant and principal	Weekly meeting*	Big events and important meetings this week	Follow-up notes and next steps for assistance
Example: Principal Angelou	Monday, May 4th at 10 a.m.	Guiding coalition meeting in office conference room	Need printed folders with benchmark data for all grades for each member and water bottles

* The weekly meeting should be calendared as a regular event between thirty to sixty minutes.
_____ date _____ set a regularly scheduled time

Figure 2.3: Administrative assistant weekly note-catcher and need-to-knows.

*Visit **go.SolutionTree.com/priorityschools** for a free reproducible version of this figure.*

Assistant Principals

The assistant principal's role can be multifaceted, encompassing student discipline, instructional leadership, and operational management. While most assistant principals tend to focus on student supervision, discipline, and operational procedures in a school setting, principals should intentionally give them instructional leadership experiences to create stronger collaborative teams and build capacity. By providing a detailed job description, a school leader ensures that the assistant principals understand expectations, including overseeing team collaborative development, fostering a positive school climate, and cultivating relationships with students and parents.

I recommend ensuring that assistant principals are not focused solely on student discipline, operations, or crisis management. At any time, an assistant principal may be asked to step in the role of interim principal and should have the opportunity to lead professional learning, facilitate or support collaborative team meetings, offer another perspective in data digs, and observe and evaluate instruction.

In the book *All Other Duties as Assigned: The Assistant Principal's Critical Role in Supporting Schools Inside and Out*, Ryan Donlan (2022) shares how the assistant principal can help support a principal by extending their reach on campus and throughout the school community. Including all administrators in discussions about teaching and learning gives more opportunities for diverse perspectives and outside experiences to be shared. In addition to the usual roles and responsibilities, assigning professional learning, learning walks, and debriefs or virtual observations through a learning library (Office of the Maricopa County School Superintendent, 2024) or Solution Tree Global PD subscription brings more enrichment to the tools of an assistant principal (Donlan, 2022).

A priority school principal should anticipate that an assistant principal may be asked to take on a principalship, temporarily or permanently, at any time. Helping assistant principals get a well-rounded experience in leadership is critical to creating sustainability in a school or district. The reality is that I have had all my assistant principals called on to take interim positions, either temporarily or leading to a permanent principal role, during my nine years in the principalship. It is a disservice to colleagues not to challenge them with new and more challenging assignments. As a leader, know that you are also responsible for growing more leaders in your organization. Invite assistant principals into difficult conversations, data digs with teacher leaders and instructional coaches, parent-teacher organizational meetings, and community partnership meetings to help grow their comfort level and expertise in those areas. All are critical to the role of the principal in a priority school.

Counselors

One of the most important and heartbreaking audits I participated in was an audit of high school transcripts that took place in 2018. The study found that in three priority high schools in Tulsa, Oklahoma, less than 40 percent of students were enrolled in the courses they needed to be college and career-ready (XQ, 2018). Of the students who did not meet the college and career readiness requirements, 16 percent of those students missed the mark by one class. The majority of those missed courses were science, computer technology, or world languages. The teacher shortage exacerbated by COVID-19 (DeCourcy & Schmitt, 2022) has made it even more challenging to staff these higher-level courses with highly qualified teachers, especially in priority schools (New Teacher Project, 2022). The New Teacher Project document provides school and district leadership with ideas to build a pipeline of teachers in school systems based on creating a route to certification for paraprofessionals in the system and also for teacher interns to work while earning certification. The state of Arizona has begun these programs to address teacher shortages, recruitment from declining college education programs, and increasing difficulty retaining high-quality teachers.

The critical link to ensure students are fulfilling the requirements they need to fulfill is the school counselor (American School Counselor Association, 2019). I learned this from Sharon Kramer when, as my coach, she asked me to make sure we had time with the counselors during each site visit, and I would follow up and monitor progress with the counselors every two weeks. Monitoring can include behavioral supports and academic interventions, depending on student needs. Learning about the transcript check process is also important for a principal in high school. Human error can lead to potentially life-changing issues for students, like missed scholarships or declined entry to college or university. Multiple transcript reviewers will increase the likelihood of catching human errors, and as instructional leaders, principals should be able to complete this critical task. The impact of counselors is great, and it's worth the time of the team to ensure that a system of checks is implemented. Plan a quarterly, half-day meeting with counselors to review transcripts and check failure rates for credit recovery planning. This should be calendared for the week after grades are submitted.

Administrative Interns

The role of an administrative intern in a school setting most commonly fulfills the intern's educational leadership master's program with one semester of practicum hours near the conclusion of the coursework (College of Community Innovation and Education, University of Central Florida, 2021). The role is an opportunity for master's degree candidates to learn in the field and allows them to work closely with a mentor who can assign appropriate tasks to fulfill the program's required hours in areas such as facilitating professional development, attending leadership meetings, shadowing an administrator during a planned emergency drill, and helping to plan a school's parent engagement event. Administrative interns are usually mentored and meet with the principal to understand the role and support the school leader's vision for the school. In the case of priority schools, I can say from personal experience that a passionate and knowledgeable administrative intern was a huge benefit to my school and leadership team. They can bring a fresh perspective and innovation to the leadership team, as well as a renewed sense of unity to a struggling team. In the case where your district does not have a job description for this role, the job description for the City of St. Charles School District (2014) offers a helpful guideline. From my own experience, key responsibilities to list include the following.

- Manage the principal's calendar, including scheduling meetings, appointments, and school events.
- Serve as a liaison between the principal and staff, students, parents, and external stakeholders.
- Prepare correspondence, reports, memos, and presentations, as directed by the principal.
- Maintain and organize records, including personnel files, student information, and school documents, in compliance with district policies.
- Coordinate and assist with event planning, such as staff meetings, parent-teacher conferences, and school ceremonies.
- Handle incoming calls, emails, and in-person inquiries and ensure prompt and courteous responses.
- Monitor and manage budgets, purchase orders, and invoices as directed by the principal.
- Assist with student and staff scheduling, including processing substitute requests and maintaining attendance records.

- Provide logistical and clerical support during emergencies, drills, or other urgent situations.
- Maintain confidentiality in all matters involving staff, students, and families.

School Resource Officer

School resource officers have become highly controversial in some school districts, as some consider them drivers of the school-to-prison pipeline (Resendes & Hinger, 2021). According to the American University School of Education (2021), 290,600 students were referred to law enforcement agencies or arrested by school-based officers during the 2015–2016 school year. Only 15 percent of students were Black, but these students represented 31 percent of law enforcement referrals and arrests. Conversely, 49 percent of students were White, but these students represented just 36 percent of law enforcement referrals or arrests. Matthew T. Theriot (2009) claims that an increase in the number of school resource officers has led to an increase in the number of arrests of students of color. In priority schools, where discipline referrals are more numerous than in other schools, in my experience, the presence of school resource officers can exacerbate volatile situations if the officer is not a part of the school community. By this, I mean that an individual who is an officer and has ties to the community (that is, they know families and parents) can be of service in deescalating situations in the school. Conversely, an individual who may not know the environment and cultural norms can certainly work against a principal who is trying to ensure compromise and restorative justice. In my experience, most site principals do not have a say in selecting their school resource officer.

Like all employees and partners, the right person makes all the difference in hiring a school resource officer. As a high school principal in a Title I school, I experienced both highly relational school resource officers who helped us work through volatile situations such as police brutality in the community and traditional disciplinarian school resource officers who did not create positive relationships with students. The difference is immense when a leader is focused on creating a school climate where students also see the school resource officer as a resource to help them understand societal crime and the implications for them as teens and as students. Research shows that school resource officers can have the opposite effect of their intent. One study finds that their presence greatly increases the use of exclusionary discipline (discipline resulting in missed school) compared to schools without them (Fisher & Hennessy, 2016).

Another study finds that the presence of a school resource officer has been associated with a practically and statistically significant increase in arrests for the subjective and minor offense of disorderly conduct. Simultaneously, school resource officers are associated with a smaller decrease in arrest rates for assault and weapons (Theriot, 2009). Lastly, an additional study finds that school resource officer presence led to higher arrest rates for ninth-grade students and those who are disruptive in school, but it notes there are overall fewer crimes reported to law enforcement in the sampled schools (Owens, 2017). School resource officers perform more law-enforcement activities in schools with higher measures of student disadvantage (Lynch, Gainey, & Chappell, 2016). In my experience, a male authority figure can exacerbate or escalate highly volatile situations if his stance is directive and imposes what students can interpret as a battle of wills. As an example, the social-emotional learning approach would be to have a confidential conversation with a student following a physical altercation to understand and unpack the context. Witnessing the opposite of a restorative practice could entail a public toe-to-toe confrontation, which puts both parties into an aggressive stance and battle of wills or egos. I have seen this type of approach have an incendiary effect in a cafeteria, hallway, or classroom. Roleplaying how a school resource officer would handle the situation can help a leader understand if their approach will enhance or diminish the school culture for students.

Conclusion

Everyone in a priority school plays a role in creating an environment that is not only conducive to learning but is also empathetic and supportive of second chances. All the roles in a school are critical, as there is usually not an abundance of adults in comparison to the students, and therefore, there is a need for efficiency and intentionality in all we do. The time one spends with their work family in school is taxing, yet from my experience, it is also very rewarding. Examining our systems through the lens of discipline data and referrals by subgroups can help us identify ways to improve our systems and undo procedures that are producing inequitable outcomes for students. Students are always watching and learning from how they see adults interacting with one another, and our relationships can help shape their behaviors and self-perceptions.

In the next chapter, I move on to how to deal with the hard conversations that are often necessary for a priority school principal's work.

Chapter 3

Hard Conversations

If a leader is committed to making long-term and sustainable changes, they have to commit to a solid number of years. In other words, they must accept that they will not achieve all of their goals in the first year. The first year is about observation and diagnosis and having hard conversations as difficult truths are uncovered. These hard truths will keep coming to the surface as time goes on. Coming into a priority school with the mindset that an outsider is needed to fix the problem will likely get a new priority school principal few followers. Transparency means sharing ideas and being open to looking at the current practices and policies that may not be working for everyone. Have hard conversations so that solutions that perpetuate problems can be discovered. Be open to feedback. Hopefully, there is time to bring people into multiple discussions to fully understand the landscape.

In my experience, new leaders tend to avoid interactions characterized by high emotions, far-reaching impact, and personal perspectives. For most people, it is instinctual to avoid confrontation, and we often view hard topics of conversation as something to avoid (Grenny, Patterson, McMillan, Switzler, & Gregory, 2021).

But leaders of priority schools don't have the luxury of hiding from hard conversations. The ability to step back and ascertain the perspectives at play, hidden agendas, and possible win-wins is a skill that they will need to develop to be successful. Ironically, my best role models for dealing with high-stakes conversations derive from examples of what I knew I did *not* want to be as a leader: reactionary, emotional, and inflammatory. Being a bystander for conversations that escalate, making time to reflect on how each side could have handled things differently, and practicing different routes to resolution provided me with opportunities to learn.

Thinking you can't do this? Think again. Having hard conversations is a skill that can be learned, and it's a skill that will serve priority principals well over and over again. Moments in which the principal is under a microscope often demand these conversations, sometimes without the chance to prepare, such as when a teacher needs help with an upset parent who confronts them during morning drop-off. Other instances might have more lead time but with much riding on your response, such as holding a teacher responsible who knowingly and repeatedly comes to collaborative team meetings late and unprepared. These moments are important not only for their immediate outcomes but for building lasting credibility and trust with the staff members, other administrators, and families. People talk. The preparation and forethought for such critical conversations can require valuable time on the front end but will pay off in the long run. And with practice, you will be able to conduct these conversations successfully on the fly.

The science behind the high-pressure conversations that can either build trust and respect or erode leadership's shaky foundation lies in our brain chemistry. The brain's responses are fight or flight in stressful situations, and high-stakes conversations certainly qualify. Our ancestors relied on these responses to stay safe from physical danger, and our brains still react the same way without distinguishing between physical, emotional, and social threats. When the brain perceives a threat, the emotional part of the brain takes over from the rational part. The body releases cortisol and adrenaline to prepare us to deal with the threat (LeWine, 2024). Psychologist and author Daniel Goleman (1995) refers to this as *amygdala hijack* in his book *Emotional Intelligence: Why It Can Matter More Than IQ*. Physical symptoms can occur, like a faster heart rate, sweating, racing thoughts, and stomach pain. When this happens, it's harder to think clearly, remember things, and control reactions. Fortunately, you can train for situations of high stress due to hard conversations. Before the talk, practice the internal dialogue of asking yourself, "What's really behind this outburst?" "Am

I seeing fear, anger, or frustration?" and "How can I extend understanding and compassion to defuse the situation and engage in meaningful discussion with this individual?"

It's not always readily apparent when a situation requires an urgent response (as in a safety situation) or when you have time to let the emotions subside before engaging. Sometimes, leaders need to make critical decisions, and rarely can they make everyone happy. Principals can help alleviate this by ascertaining the levels of loss that stakeholders may feel and being prepared to explain the reasons behind the decision. For example, leaders must balance their duties with professional growth by occasionally attending conferences, which means running the risk of being away during an emergency. It's challenging to control the feelings of fear, guilt, and shame when something happens and you are gone. No one can be everywhere at once, and something will inevitably happen while you're away.

This chapter offers ways to apply these strategies before and during hard conversations about ensuring accountability at every level and offers a process for holding high-stakes conversations.

Accountability at Every Level

In the book *Crucial Accountability: Tools for Resolving Violated Expectations, Broken Commitments, and Bad Behavior* (Patterson, Grenny, Maxfield, McMillan, & Switzler, 2013), the authors state, "All accountability discussions start with the question, 'Why didn't you keep your commitment?'" (p. 2). In my career of working with teachers, teacher leaders, and administrators in schools, I have experienced the need to ask that question at every level of the organization. In fact, I tell my teams that the fastest way to build trust is listening and following through on what you said you were going to do.

And yet, accountability seems to also be one of the most difficult aspects of the job, either because of a lack of organized follow-up as part of the reflection cycle or a tendency to overpromise. When we don't follow through, people notice: Parents complain of never getting a follow-up call or email, students complain about rewards that never materialize, and administrators become frustrated when district leadership does not deliver on consequences, curriculum, or other supports. In a collaborative team, failed commitments can mean ongoing struggles for new teachers who haven't been properly onboarded into the PLC process and received necessary instructional coaching. The power of teams is the mutual accountability they promise to fulfill through common commitments.

As discussed in chapter 1 (page 5), individuals need to be able to embrace these commitments and understand the purpose and vision of the school that teams commit to uphold through their work. Therefore, the foundation of accountability is a common understanding of the vision and the why behind the work of collaborative teams. A leader or team must engage in the process of visioning and backward planning for the actions and roles that will be necessary to achieve their end goal. The school's mission, vision, commitments, and goals provide a foundation and common ground for hard conversations.

Clarity of the steps to achieve the vision through the mission leads directly to action planning and role clarity for team members. Like a living organism, if one part of the interdependent team fails to live up to its commitments, that failure interferes with the instructional cycle, which negatively impacts student learning. Conversations around accountability need to be documented with due dates and action steps, along with the names of the team members who will perform them. These should be shared with everyone involved. Keeping agendas and meeting minutes allows for mutual accountability. One way that your school superstars get burned out is when a team member continually violates the collective commitments or meeting norms. As leaders, we must be aware that repeatedly going to the same hard-working people can wear them down and diminish their capacity and willingness to volunteer when help is needed. The leader, often a teacher leader or department head, feels a lack of respect when this happens. Consequently, discussions around accountability are at risk of becoming personal and accusatory instead of professional. In preparing for these conversations, be specific and prepared with the signed meeting agendas and due dates. Figure 3.1 is an example of a meeting agenda to stay on topic.

Professional Learning Communities Overview

Team: _____ Date: _____

"A professional learning community is an ongoing process in which educators work in recurring cycles of collective inquiry and action research to increase their learning and the learning of the students they serve" (DuFour et al., 2024, p. 2).

Four Critical Questions

1. What do we want students to learn?
2. How will we know if they have learned?
3. What will we do if they don't learn?
4. What will we do if they already know it?

Three Big Ideas
1. Focus on learning
2. Collaboration
3. Focus on results

Team Topics
- ☐ SMART goals
- ☐ Collaboration to create common assessments
- ☐ Discussion of data from common assessments or benchmarks following the data-analysis protocol
- ☐ Lesson plans
- ☐ Instructional strategies or techniques
- ☐ Use of technology within the curriculum
- ☐ Methods to remediate and enrich
- ☐ Ways to use differentiated instruction
- ☐ Ways to use collaborative learning
- ☐ Interventions for students at risk of not meeting proficiency goals
- ☐ Goals to improve team and individual professional development
- ☐ Common procedures and protocols to support student learning
- ☐ Instructional focus walks
- ☐ Scope and sequence; pacing

Figure 3.1: Collaborative team agenda example.

*Visit **go.SolutionTree.com/priorityschools** for a free reproducible version of this figure.*

No collaborative team could cover all the items on this agenda in a single meeting, but the purpose of listing all the items is to keep the team from going off task. When topics don't get covered in one meeting, they roll over to the next. This emphasizes the cyclical and ongoing nature of the work in a PLC.

My experience with teams in priority schools has shown me that the hard conversations arising from data review make teachers unwilling to discuss them. In schools with one teacher per grade per subject, they may feel they are being singled out or identified. Low proficiency numbers feel daunting to tackle and impossible to improve. A priority school likely has years of underperformance that has contributed to a feeling of hopelessness among teachers and students. The good news is that a priority school leader can center the right conversations and emphasize that improved student learning is an attainable goal that everyone can unite behind. To facilitate difficult team discussions around these topics, each team member will complete an individual data-analysis protocol (see figure 3.2, page 70).

Data-Analysis Protocol

Team: _____

Teachers: _____ Date: _____

The following analysis is based on our team's common assessment of the following standards.

1. _____
2. _____
3. _____

Which of our students needs additional time and support to achieve at or above proficiency on the standards? Include the specific standards with each student's name.

_____
_____
_____

On which standards did my students perform the lowest?

_____
_____
_____

What strategies were used by teammates whose students performed well?

_____
_____
_____

On which standards did all students perform poorly?

_____
_____
_____

What do we believe is the cause? What is the misconception?

_____
_____
_____

What is our plan for improving results?

_____
_____
_____

How will we provide that time and support? Be specific.

For example, students who did not show proficiency in standard 2.3 will receive instruction from Ms. Smith, who had the highest number of passing students on the standard.

_____
_____
_____
_____
_____

| **What is our plan to enrich and extend the learning for students who are highly proficient? Be specific.** |
| *For example, students attend Ms. Jones' class, where they will extend their understanding by working in teams on an application scenario.* |
| _____ |
| _____ |
| _____ |
| _____ |
| _____ |

Figure 3.2: Data-analysis protocol.

*Visit **go.SolutionTree.com/priorityschools** for a free reproducible version of this figure.*

To help maximize time during collaborative team meetings, some of the questions on the data-analysis protocol should be answered prior to the team discussion. For example, while the team determines together which standards to evaluate on each assessment, individual teachers should include their students' results (from student data and information platform) with individual names and standards. They should also note on which standards their students scored the lowest. Again, this is a vulnerable moment for many teachers. Teams that have embodied the collaborative culture of a PLC will have more success with the rich discussion opportunities that analyzing data provides. Teachers whose students are struggling may discover a game-changing instructional strategy from other teachers with students who are performing well.

For any standards with which all students had poor performance, the team can collectively discuss possible causes of the problem. This, too, can be a difficult conversation, but by focusing on the why, teams can move forward. Team members might talk about the need for different instructional strategies, different resources, better scaffolding, and more. From there, they can plan how to improve student performance. How will they reteach or reinforce? What strategies will they use? What materials will they need?

Reinforcement means that learning targets and standards that we know are foundational and needed for upcoming units should be continually reiterated for stronger conceptual understanding. Sometimes, reinforcement can be intertwined with upcoming standards, and at other times, learning targets and standards must be retaught. In the acceleration model (Kramer & Schuhl, 2017), the continuous spiraling of essential and lasting standards is a key component to filling in gaps without the unattainable task of filling in a year's worth of curriculum or more. Teachers should focus on multiple exposures to critical content that is necessary for scaffolded learning. They must also consider how to differentiate to meet the needs of all students, including the possibility of reorganizing classes to help manage students performing at different levels. While the focus is on current students, teachers can also give some thought to what they can do differently next time when introducing each standard. Next, the team can consider how it will meet the needs of highly proficient students. What type of enrichment will team members use?

Following the protocol means that collaborative team time does not become a time to focus on conversations outside of learning. It is intended to help teachers analyze student mastery by standard and plan for intervention time so that, ultimately all students have mastery of the identified essential standards.

I created the tool in figure 3.3 for teams of teachers and administrators to ensure that we all had accountability and clarity around what would be monitored and, therefore, what was most important. As a new priority school principal, I quickly found out two things: (1) I had few proven tools in my toolbelt outside of working the four critical questions around student learning, and (2) I knew if I didn't make it clear and explicit what needed to be done, by when, and who should be doing it, it would not be done at all. The tool in this form is what worked in my context, but leaders can adapt it to use it in their own buildings.

Collaborative Tasks and Products

NOTE: All bolded products or artifacts require a specific schoolwide form.

Defined Tasks	Due Date	Product or Artifact	Responsible Party	Submit Product To (Accountability)
Create and continuously evaluate team norms	Leadership teams 6/4 9/____ for Grade-Level Content 9/____ Vertical	**Academic content team and grade-level content teams**	Leadership team and team leaders	Principal Assistant principal
Establish team SMART goals	Leadership site teams 6/4	**SMART goal worksheet**	All members	Team leads to leadership teams
Identify professional development needs based on SMART goals	Ongoing		Principal	Principal
Identify essential standards	Ongoing	List of essential standards	All members	All teachers Team leads

Update student trackers	Ongoing in classrooms	**Implementation readiness checkup**		Team leads
Maintain protocols for agendas, record keeping, minutes, consensus, roles, and so on	Each team meeting; ongoing	**Google Docs shared team binder**	Agenda and minutes	Store all documents in the team Google binder
Reflect on lesson plans	Weekly for September	**Reflection template**	All members; as assigned	Principal
Develop common mini-assessments with scoring guide	Coincide with tracker implementation Update _____ / _____	Common assessment	All members with like partner teacher	Team leads
Analyze assessment results of common assessments	Ongoing with mini-assessment implementation		All members	Live binder
Identify systematic responses for students who are failing or fail assessments	After trackers or mini-assessments are implemented	Interventions with options for make-ups, student-specific data by standard	All members	Document through agendas and minutes
Identify systematic responses for students who have already mastered objectives	Every two weeks	Options for enrichment with curriculum extensions	All members	Document through agendas and minutes
Evaluate progress on SMART goals for Forward data	Fall 20_____, Winter 20_____, Spring 20_____	**SMART goal worksheet**	All members	Site teams Leadership team Live binders

Figure 3.3: Collaborative tasks and products.

*Visit **go.SolutionTree.com/priorityschools** for a free reproducible version of this figure.*

Elements that you may choose to include are some of the constants.

- We create SMART goals to keep us accountable (specific, measurable, achievable, results oriented, and time bound; Conzemius & O'Neill, 2014). See figure 3.4 (page 74) for a useful template and example.

- We create team norms to guide our behaviors and hold each other accountable to the focus of our work: student learning. Inevitably, there will be disagreements. Predetermined norms help redirect the team when emotions run high.

SMART goal: At least 50 percent of all ninth graders will be proficient in operations of positive and negative numbers, fractions, and solving an equation for a variable.

School year: 2023-2024

Department: Mathematics   Team: Algebra I teachers

Team leader: Team members:

Identify a student achievement SMART goal
(strategic and specific, measurable, attainable, results oriented, and time bound):

Students will show incremental growth on common formative assessments leading up to the summative assessment (first nine weeks).

Action Steps and Products	Team Members	Time Frame	Results and Evaluation
What steps or activities will you initiate to achieve your goals? What products will you create?	Who is responsible for initiating or sustaining the action step or product?	What is a realistic time frame for each step or product?	How will you assess your progress? What evidence will you use to show you are making progress?
Identify all previous essential standards to support the goal. Create common formative assessments to measure growth in intervention sessions.	Algebra I team	One week	Common formative assessments for ongoing growth measurement during the flex time intervention and Tier 2 in class small groups.
Create bellringer five-minute activities to engage students with prior content and preview learning.	Algebra I team	Ongoing for the quarter	Bellringers will help teachers formatively assess mastery and prepare for instructional moves and small groups.
Access hands-on manipulatives and mathematics games.	Instructional coach	Ongoing for the quarter	Increase successful engagement with mathematics areas of growth to increase mastery.

Source: Adapted from Buffum & Mattos, 2020.
Figure 3.4: SMART goal template.

Visit **go.SolutionTree.com/priorityschools** *for a free reproducible version of this figure.*

- Essential standards help teachers focus on what we have agreed are standards that have readiness, endurance, can be assessed, and have leverage (REAL; Many, Maffoni, Sparks, & Thomas, 2022).

- Student trackers gamify data for students. I used simple bar graphs for three to five essential standards and had students color in their level of mastery as their proficiency grew. They were competitive with themselves and across classrooms. This created momentum and positive energy about learning. In priority schools, it can be hard to counter the attitude that being smart isn't cool, but gamifying the process of learning engages students in a fun way. It naturally leads to opportunities for intervention and celebrations.

- Common formative mini-assessments are, ideally, quick check-ins to assess learning that can be done on the same day across two or more subjects and grade levels. This informs teachers about which strategies are working and helps uncover successful practices across classrooms. These assessments comprise three to five questions and help guide planning for interventions or extensions.

Keeping the highest priority items in priority schools at the forefront for collaborative teacher teams can be difficult. The collaborative tasks tool was my way of saying, "Here's what I will be looking for as artifacts of our collective work measuring students' learning." How a priority school leader chooses to express this idea can vary, but the message should be consistent. Because teams had clarity about expectations and the reasons behind them, discussions might have been difficult, but they were productive.

High-Stakes Conversations

There comes a time for every school leader when they must engage in hard conversations that are highly likely to be unwelcome and uncomfortable for everyone involved. For example, perhaps you need to move a teacher to a different physical location or content area, or you may have to implement a plan of improvement with a staff member who is struggling.

Moving Personnel

There are inevitably times when the principal must move a teacher to a different content area or classroom space based on assessment data or student needs. Teachers take a lot of time and care in the preparation of their classrooms to create flow or support the activities that enable them to best deliver the curriculum. A change, especially for a teacher who has not experienced such a move, can feel traumatic. The priority school leader should expect some resistance in these instances and, therefore, prepare for a hard conversation. This is essentially managing change.

In my experience, even if the principal has the data to support a move, it becomes personal because of teachers' attachment to the classroom and their setup. They may have years of collected materials or other variables like windows, proximity to the restroom, or a neighboring teacher friend. In the cases where adult drama overtakes what seems like a straightforward logistical decision, the leader needs to maintain calm, go back to the why, and refer to the assessment data or student needs. Watching body language and listening to the reaction of the teacher are clues to help understand the teacher's motivation and perspective. If data are below expectations, it may mean the principal must remove the teacher from a tested area. Since No Child Left Behind was enacted in 2001, educators have been measured on proficiency and growth in key content areas. This is out of our control, and as leaders, we need to ensure the strongest teachers are assigned to those areas; it affects the school's rating, often funding from federal and state sources, and most importantly, the perception of efficacy for students, families, faculty, and staff. Be prepared to keep the conversation objective, unemotional, and professional. Plan to have this conversation in a safe, one-on-one meeting. If after a teacher has been supported with a growth plan, instructional coaching, and feedback from walkthroughs to make improvements but with limited progress, then a move might be inevitable.

Plans of Improvement

Plans of improvement are tied to specific domains in the district evaluation tool in most cases; however, I have created my own with the help of colleagues in two large districts that did not have a formal instrument-aligned template. As a principal, you must have documentation of specific instances of behavioral, procedural, or performance violations noted with dates and times. Whether the areas needing improvement are professional duties and responsibilities or instruction, they must clearly correlate to the claims of subpar results. For example, if a teacher is violating the school grading policy of not weighing homework above 10 percent of the grade, as a principal, be specific about why this violation matters.

First, many students in priority schools may also be caregivers for younger siblings or other family members, hindering them from being able to stay for extra support after school. Second, we have no certainty that the student is the one completing the work. A student may have a friend, peer, sibling, parent, or technology helping to complete their work. With readily available programs, I have seen this becoming more widespread and impacting the validity of student homework. Finally, if a student is in a home without power or internet, they may not be able to complete the work, and a highly weighted homework category can limit the growth in data regardless of whether they have mastered the content.

The more opportunities for feedback, the better. A teacher who is struggling may try to claim it's an isolated incident if the school leader is rarely in the classroom or only comes by during formal evaluations. Using sticky notes or short emails can be an effective, nonthreatening way to relate some of your concerns or highlights to the teacher and support reflective growth.

Just as teachers do for students, leaders have a responsibility to help educators understand the unintended consequences of some practices. I find that there is rarely malicious intent in many practices in schools; it is merely that teachers are replicating what they experienced or were taught by a mentor teacher. This is why feedback that is ongoing and unemotional is important. Be thoughtful and give specific examples of the impact on students. If a teacher violates the professional dress code, you may simply need to cite the school's policy—quite different in results and feedback when dealing with a sensitive matter versus a practical matter. For the most part, the more frequently a priority school principal visits classrooms and leaves a positive note, the more accepting a teacher will be of growth recommendations about important factors that impact student learning.

A plan for improvement can be aligned with performance, behavior, or policy. As such, a priority school leader needs to be knowledgeable about the teacher contract, district and school policy, and teacher handbook of expectations. I created the growth plan in figure 3.5 (page 78) based on the idea that, for the most part, everyone wants to feel successful in their job and may need support to get there. It is a template that can be used or revised if your district doesn't have a standard template for improvement.

I see the need for improvement plans in large urban priority schools as well as small rural districts. My rule is that the first infraction should always trigger a discussion. The second should result in a discussion with a written follow-up. Depending on the nature of the circumstances, this might also include a written reprimand. The third infraction necessitates a plan for improvement with a timeline for check-ins on progress, support, and possible training.

Letter for Plan of Improvement

Date: _____ Method of delivery: _____

Personal and Confidential

To: _____ From: _____

Subject: Meeting summary with directives

cc: Human Resources

Following is a summary of the due process meeting held on _____ at _____ regarding the following policies.

_____
_____
_____

During the meeting, we discussed the following.

_____
_____
_____

Regarding the stated discussion, you stated the following.

_____
_____
_____

I offered you the following assistance and guidance.

_____
_____
_____

During the meeting, you were directed to take the following action steps.

_____
_____
_____

Keep the content of this conversation confidential. Specifically, do not share the content of this conversation with others involved in this incident. Doing so could be considered retaliation and would be subject to additional disciplinary action.

Please be advised that repeated violations of misconduct will result in further disciplinary action up to and including dismissal.

If this letter does not reflect your recollection, please notify me in writing by _____. Otherwise, I shall assume this to be an accurate summary of our conference.

_____   _____
Signature of Employee   Date

Your signature indicates that you received, read, and understand this memo.

Figure 3.5: Letter for a plan of improvement.

*Visit **go.SolutionTree.com/priorityschools** for a free reproducible version of this figure.*

I created the template in figure 3.6 to correlate directly with the evaluation instrument, which has indicators to look for during an observation. It can be helpful to revise the verbiage below to align with any language in the evaluation instrument used at your school or district.

Teacher Improvement Plan

Teacher: _____ Initiator of Plan: _____

Date of Beginning of Plan: _____ End of 45 days: _____

Goal:

Educator will . . . (add desired outcome using evaluation or policy language)

_____
_____
_____
_____
_____

Evidence goal is met:

Data collected from informal and formal classroom observations

Submitted daily lesson plans (add template name) _____

Documented assessment data in (add platform) _____

No further student or family complaints regarding (add incident topic) _____

Teacher Expectations			
Area Needing Improvement	**Suggested Actions and Evidence** *(Include the responsible party in description)*	**Resources**	**Scheduled Progress Monitoring and Completion Dates**
Timely lesson planning and instructional strategies should be shared with collaborative teams and in professional development. Lesson plans should be the observed experience in the classroom and match district pacing to cover the adopted curriculum. Plans should include student engagement strategies and formative assessment. Lastly, Tier 2 small group instruction should be included.	Team agendas for identifying standards, creating targets, and using common formative assessments. Team agendas for discussion and lesson plan creation based on essential standards.	State standards Essential standards and pacing guide from district instructional coaches Instructional coaches model engagement activities and provide manipulatives.	Weekly classroom observations (informal) throughout a forty-five-day period, with the exception of the week the formal observation occurs. Formal classroom observation cycle completed by [date]. Coach to teacher feedback on lesson delivery.

Figure 3.6: Educator improvement plan template.

continued →

		Lesson plan template Observation instrument for reference on evaluative instructional elements	Complete lesson plans that contain a minimum of one week at a time. Weekly classroom observations (informal) completed throughout a forty-five-day period ending [date]. Formal classroom observation cycle completed by [date].
Development or selection and use of valid, real-time, and summative assessments aligned to learning objectives used for the reliable measurement of learning outcomes.	Evidence will include assessments (either teacher-developed or selected premade assessments from viable, administration approved resources) aligned to learning objectives and submitted lesson plans.	Assessment bank Observation instrument regarding assessment	Real-time assessments should be provided with each daily lesson submitted for review and approval by administration. Summative assessments should be provided with each learning unit submitted for review and approval by administration.

This plan will be monitored as outlined in the Scheduled Progress Monitoring column.

Accompanying this plan is the preliminary notice of inadequacy of classroom performance required by (add state statute) _____. Failure to meet expectations in the focus areas above within forty-five (45) instructional days may result in not receiving a contract for (add school year) _____, removal from teaching position, and/or termination.

Based on your efforts, I am prepared to assist you in meeting the expectations of this plan.

_____   _____
Supervising administrator: **Date:**

I am aware of this plan, and I intend to follow through with the suggested actions and utilize all available resources.

_____   _____
Employee: **Date:**

I am aware an improvement plan has been developed for the certified employee named here and will participate in progress monitoring and development.

_____   _____
District administrator: **Date:**

The teacher's signature denotes receipt of the form and acknowledgment that the evaluator has notified the employee of unacceptable performance.

*Visit **go.SolutionTree.com/priorityschools** for a free reproducible version of this figure.*

A principal might use this improvement plan with, for example, a special education teacher who is not following the accommodations or modifications in a student's individualized education program (IEP). The artifacts of improvement could be lesson plans that specify the instructional modifications the teacher is going to use to meet IEP requirements. The data evidence could be improved learning or engagement on the part of the student. The supports provided could be to mentor the special education teacher's guidance or additional training from a district or regional special education provider. Lastly, retraining could be required on the IEP documentation platform or monitoring of the teacher's student case files for evidence of needed modifications and differentiation for students on the caseload.

Principals should always emphasize that growth is the goal. Therefore, practice noting when an improvement has been accomplished. This indicates encouragement for the educator and hopefully motivation to make the new habits the new norm. The template in figure 3.7 can be revised to be appropriate for the context of the improvement plan.

Improvement Plan—*Final Comments and Closure Will Be Underlined*

Recipient: _____ **Initiator of Plan:** _____

Evidence goal is met:

Formal and informal observations

List all areas and outcomes from the original template.

_____
_____
_____
_____
_____

Goal:

Educator will . . . (add desired outcome in evaluation or policy language)

_____
_____
_____
_____
_____

Figure 3.7: Follow-up to an educator improvement plan or conclusion letter.

continued →

Evidence goal is met:

Data collected from informal and formal classroom observations.

Submitted daily lesson plans (add template name) _____

Documented assessment data in (add platform) _____

No further student or family complaints regarding (add incident topic) _____

Teacher Expectations			
Area Needing Improvement	**Suggested Actions and Evidence** *(Include the responsible party in description)*	**Resources**	**Scheduled Progress Monitoring and Completion Dates**
Lesson planning and instructional strategies shared with collaborative teams and in professional development.	Classroom observations Coach's log	Outcome from support High-impact instructional strategies, Hattie Weekly coaching with assigned instructional coach	Weekly classroom observations (informal) throughout a forty-five-day period, with the exception of the week the formal observation occurs. Formal classroom observation cycle completed by [date]. Add results

Accompanying this plan is the Preliminary Notice of Inadequacy of Classroom Performance required by ARS §15-538 et seq. Failure to meet expectations in the focus areas above within forty-five (45) instructional days may result in removal from position and/or termination.

Based on the incomplete directives listed above, this document serves as notification of a successfully completed growth plan (add date and signature).

Based on the incomplete directives listed above, this document serves as notification of contract non-renewal for the _____ school year; in addition to the attached disciplinary reprimand and notice of non-negotiable administrative leave for ten (10) days.

I acknowledge receipt of the outcomes of this plan for improvement.

_____

Employee: **Date:**

I am aware an improvement plan has been developed for the certified employee named here and will participate in progress monitoring and development.

_____

District administrator: **Date:**

The employee's signature denotes receipt of the form and acknowledgment that the evaluator has notified the employee of the results of the plan.

Some educators assume that an improvement plan is a message to move on. If growth or improvement plans are rare or have preceded a teacher's exodus, especially in a priority school, this can be interpreted as an exit rather than a support with the hope of successful growth. As priority school leaders, we have a responsibility to sow the seeds of hope in many places—for students, for teachers, for the community, and for the future. If we don't believe that growth is possible, then in my mind, that idea is fundamentally opposed to our purpose, which is to increase learning to impact lives in a positive way. Everyone can learn and improve, whether they're students or teachers. Once again, the difficult conversations that arise from improvement plans come back to the *why*.

A Process for Holding Hard Conversations

When holding especially hard conversations, I turn to a method based on the book *Crucial Conversations: Tools for Talking When Stakes Are High* (Grenny et al., 2021). According to Grenny and his colleagues (2021), a *crucial conversation* is a high-stakes, emotional discussion with opposing opinions and a risk of negative outcomes. Priority school principals are likely to recognize these attributes in many of the hard conversations they must engage in throughout the school year. But, as discussed in the opening of this chapter, you can prepare for these conversations. Grenny and his colleagues (2021) lay out the process for holding hard conversations, which I have adapted as follows.

1. **Know the purpose of the conversation:** Understand the outcome you would like to achieve from the conversation and plan backward to make a strong argument starting with the why. Help make a compelling, persuasive argument through policy or a moral imperative.

2. **Summarize the current situation:** Sequentially state the events that created the current scenario. Give the implications for the students, teachers, teams, and the larger organization. Outline the pros and cons with possible outcomes.

3. **Identify the problem:** Reiterate the root cause problem or issue that needs to be solved or rectified.

4. **Communicate expectations:** Give the expected behaviors to rectify the situation, including meetings, messages, and written documentation. Give a step-by-step account of how you would like to see the situation remedied, citing policy or best practices adopted by the school or district.

5. **Listen to explanations:** Be open to hearing perspectives and motivation. This will help you come together to craft a solution.

6. **Work on solutions:** If time permits, give the employee time to process and ask questions. Give yourself time to process and find other more subtle solutions.

7. **Devise action steps:** Follow up the verbal discussion with written step-by-step sequential documentation. Include possible verbiage and timelines.

8. **Agree on a goal:** In writing and verbally, refer back to the shared end goal. The action steps should lead to the goal's attainment.

9. **Hold everyone accountable:** Follow up and request updates. Have a debriefing meeting once the problem is solved to set expectations for future behaviors. If there is no follow-through on the plan originally shared in the conversation, you may need to move forward with disciplinary action in addition to the corrective actions that were agreed upon.

Figure 3.8 offers a condensed worksheet template to work through the process of hard conversations.

Meeting Step	
Purpose *We are meeting today to discuss a solution that ensures all students have a teacher in the classroom when they arrive at school at 8:15.*	The outcome would be that the employee has an opportunity to explain their circumstances that cause tardiness, but ultimately every class is supervised on time.
Current Situation *Other staff members are covering your class in the mornings if you are not on campus.*	
Problem *Students deserve the opportunity to have breakfast and to complete their morning work in their classroom with their teacher present.*	
Expectations *The handbook states that all employees will arrive to campus thirty minutes prior to the start of the school day.*	
Explanation *Tell me why it is a struggle to be at work by 8:15.*	

Solution *How can you find a solution that supports the expectations and considers the best interest of the students?*	
Action Steps *What action steps are necessary to implement the solution?*	
Goal *SMART goal*	
Accountability *How will you monitor progress toward the goal?*	

Source: © 2022 by Holly Diaz, Ace Educators, LLC. Used with permission.
Figure 3.8: Hard conversation worksheet.

Conclusion

In this chapter, I have focused on recommendations for framing and preparing for hard conversations, including accountability conversations within teams, some insight into how and when to hold conversations about personnel moves, methods of documenting improvement plans that have worked for me in large and small schools and districts, and a process for holding the most high-stakes conversations. Delivery is just as important as content in sensitive conversations. Follow up verbal meetings with written accounts of the discussion. Just as planning for these conversations is critical to success, reflection on the outcome is also important to improving difficult conversations.

Chapter 4

Visibility and Communication

High visibility for a priority school principal is a necessity because they symbolize stability, consistency, and accountability in a school. Priority schools often have a poor reputation in the community, which can hinder student success. Getting into the community to create positive relationships with families and influential leaders can be an avenue to strengthen the community's perception of the school. Trust between the school and families has likely been damaged, but time, effort, follow-through, and transparency can rebuild it.

High visibility is paramount for the success of a principal in a priority school; just as teachers appear at their classroom door in the morning and between classes in the hallway, so do principals need to model the behavior. Through a proactive and visible approach, priority school principals can meet the diverse demands of their role, promote student achievement, and advocate for their school community's needs. Educational leaders need to recognize the significance of high visibility as a tool for success.

Knowing the context and culture of a school community is a priority for a school principal to be able to communicate clearly and effectively with the community.

As an assistant principal, I witnessed the priority school principal in a parent-and-student assembly take off his designer loafer, raise it above his head, and say to the audience, "Most of you cannot afford one of my shoes, let alone both of them. If you don't get serious about your education, you will never afford to get out of here." I was shocked. Families walked out. That priority school principal did not make it to the end of the year.

Visibility doesn't just mean being seen; it also means clear communication. The benefits of effective communication for principals in priority schools are immeasurable.

- **Trust and relationships:** With consistent, honest communication, principals build trust and positive relationships with students, staff, parents, and community members. It may take time, but when stakeholders begin to see that they can expect regularity and transparency, they feel valued.

- **Conflict resolution:** By promoting open and honest communication, principals can help resolve conflicts and address issues promptly. This minimizes disruptions to the learning environment and fosters a sense of fairness and understanding.

- **Engaging stakeholders:** Effective communication allows principals to engage stakeholders such as teachers, parents, and community members in decision-making processes. Involving them in school initiatives and seeking their input creates ownership and supports a collaborative culture.

- **Sharing goals and expectations:** Principals can ensure that the school's mission, vision, and commitments or norms are known and honored throughout the school and the community, aligning everyone toward a common purpose. This means that everyone understands what is expected of them and works together toward achieving shared objectives.

- **Celebrating achievements:** A hallmark of PLCs is celebrations, big and small. Principals can use effective communication to highlight and celebrate student and staff achievements. Recognizing and sharing successes not only boosts morale but also reinforces a culture of excellence and continuous improvement.

- **Addressing concerns and feedback:** Principals who actively listen and respond to concerns and feedback from stakeholders can address issues promptly and make necessary improvements.

> This demonstrates responsiveness and a commitment to continuous growth.

In an organization where people of various backgrounds, experiences, and opinions work together, effective communication is a vital tool for school leaders to create a positive culture, engage stakeholders, and enhance academic outcomes. By investing in clear and concise communication strategies, principals can foster an environment conducive to student success and community support. This might include a weekly newsletter, weekly social media updates, and agreed-on communication for high-priority FYIs. Regarding faculty feedback, an open-door policy may get overwhelming in a priority school, therefore, consider a faculty advisory committee that takes staff suggestions, weighs the pros and cons, and proposes a procedure or process to the administration. This is a clear avenue for making suggested changes through a vetting committee.

Community Support

It is difficult to turn around a priority school, but it is impossible without some community and parental support. Understanding that every parent wants their child to be successful is a starting point for a conversation and will help a leader make more progress than sarcasm, anger, or condescension. Talk to people before you talk to people; ask your administrative assistant, office manager, or teachers about the school community and local organizations that might be good resources. Take the time to prepare for conversations by knowing your context.

Regularly scheduled events and celebrations publicize achievements and mark small victories. A coffee time or virtual open office time can help a principal in a priority school gain support. Opportunities to volunteer at events and organizations in the community can also be successful. Ask your veteran staff about community hubs, meeting places, or recreational centers. Look up their calendar of events and try to attend one per quarter. Stakeholders will take note! Two concrete opportunities to interact with the community in positive ways are through the student enrollment process and engaging stakeholders online.

Understanding the Importance of a Detailed Student Enrollment Process

As school leaders strive to optimize their organization, it is crucial to establish a visible and easily understandable student enrollment process. Enrollment process clarity affects funding, student data and confidentiality, and the vertical articulation of communication as students progress through the grade levels.

If you are looking for ways to connect with the greater community, looking at your enrollment process is worth your time. The backward planning process can serve as guidance to create, review, or update an enrollment process. First, you'll need to articulate the necessary documentation required by your state. A sample checklist from my district in Arizona (Nadaburg Unified School District 81, 2024) is constructed as follows.

1. Enrollment packet (includes parent or caregiver information, emergency contacts, home language survey, exceptional student services survey, medical history information, request for records from previous school, and transferring transcript)
2. Birth certificate or affidavit
3. Proof of immunizations
4. Proof of residency (utility bill, rental agreement, any mailer with your name and address)
5. Driver's License or state-issued ID
6. Name and address of previous schools and withdrawal form
7. Proof of legal custody (if applicable)
8. IEP or 504 records (if applicable)
9. McKinney-Vento form (if applicable)

Creating a Flowchart

A *flowchart* is a visual representation of a sequential process, illustrating the steps and decision points involved. It provides a simplified overview of the student enrollment process, making it easier for all stakeholders to comprehend and follow (Li, 2016). To create an effective flowchart for staff or parents and guardians, follow these steps.

1. **Identify the key steps:** Begin by outlining the main stages of the enrollment process, such as application submission, document verification, eligibility determination, and acceptance notification.
2. **Define decision points:** Within each stage, identify decision points, such as deadlines, eligibility criteria, and potential outcomes. These decision points will determine the flow of the process.
3. **Sequence the steps:** Arrange the steps in a reasonable order, ensuring that each one follows the previous step logically. This sequencing is vital to maintain clarity and avoid confusion.

4. **Use standardized symbols:** Employ standardized symbols for differentiating process steps, decisions, and outcomes. For example, rectangles can represent process steps, diamonds for decision points, and arrows for connections.

Figure 4.1 provides an example of an enrollment process flowchart.

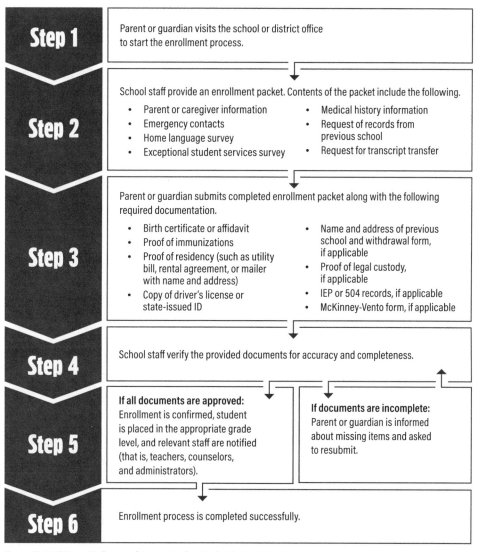

Source: © 2024 Desere Hockman and Aspasia Angelou. Used with permission.
Figure 4.1: Enrollment flowchart example.

Communicating the Flowchart

Once the flowchart is created, communicate it effectively to all stakeholders involved in the enrollment process. Consider the following strategies.

- **Use clear language:** Ensure that the flowchart is accompanied by a detailed description of each step, clearly explaining the purpose and expectations associated with it. Use simple, concise language to enhance comprehension.

- **Make it accessible:** Share the flowchart and accompanying information through multiple channels, such as the school's website, social media platforms, and informational brochures. Consider offering translations with visual prompts to clarify the steps.

- **Seek feedback:** Encourage families, students, and staff to provide feedback on the clarity and effectiveness of the flowchart. This iterative process will help identify areas that require improvement and refine the enrollment process further.

Designing a detailed student enrollment process and effectively communicating it through a flowchart can significantly enhance transparency, efficiency, and stakeholder satisfaction in priority schools. Tools like the flowchart can help a principal relieve parent anxiety during the enrollment process and make the process more efficient for the staff involved.

Tools for Engaging Stakeholders Online

Several online tools can help engage community and school stakeholders so that transportation, work schedules, and other factors are not barriers to feedback. The set of tools included in this section may increase your ability to effectively use social media for proactive communication with innovative avenues, ideas for creating websites, and polling opportunities.

When I first came into my principalship role, I was told that our community chose to communicate on social media, and therefore, it was expected that I also engage on particular platforms. This can take on a life of its own if you don't have clear parameters around topics and verbiage for the school or district page. The tools listed in table 4.1 are meant to promote positive engagement and limit the back and forth arguing that can ensue on social media.

Table 4.1: Tools for Engaging Stakeholders Online

Virtual Meeting Engagement Tools		
Tools	**Features and Functionality**	**Example Uses**
PollEverywhere	PollEverywhere is an online application that allows users to create and present digital polls, quizzes, and contests within meetings. Users can embed questions and real-time results into PowerPoint presentations and initiate them from a smartphone. Participants in meetings and presentations can respond via a computer, tablet, or smartphone browser, or they can submit responses via SMS message.	Create teams from individuals attending a webinar and use the Competitions feature to pit those teams against each other in a digital scavenger hunt. Teams must find information online related to the presentation and respond via PollEverywhere before other teams to win.
Mentimeter	Mentimeter is an online application that allows users to facilitate interactive polling and voting. It provides a variety of polling options and allows user to embed innovative, animated data displays in PowerPoint presentations. Users can vote and respond via smartphone browsers.	Set up pretest before covering content in a webinar, present the content, and then ask users to respond to a post test. Use the animated data display to demonstrate how responses changed based on the information presented.
Prezi	Prezi is a digital presentation tool, similar to PowerPoint, but designed to be more visually oriented, conversational, and interactive. With both free and non-negotiable plans, Prezi offers cloud-based and desktop applications, mobile delivery of presentations, and engagement analytics.	Use Prezi's storytelling template to present an interactive, engaging story of a program implementation.
Add-Ons for Google Slides	Add-ons are modules that users can install to add features and functionality to Google Drive applications such as Docs, Sheets, and Slides. Add-ons for slides allow presenters to easily insert quizzes and assessments, audio or video content, interactive charts, and innovative design elements directly to a Google Slides presentation.	Use Google Slides to record and present (asynchronously) content required for a certification or compliance exercise. Use an assessment add-on to build a quiz at the end of the presentation and collect performance results.
LiveWeb	LiveWeb allows users to add live web pages into a PowerPoint slide and refresh the pages real-time during the presentation. LiveWeb eliminates the need to click between a presentation and a browser window when demonstrating a website.	Provide a how-to demonstration of an interactive web form during your presentation by embedding the page with LiveWeb and completing the form without leaving your presentation.

continued →

Social Media Tools		
Tools	**Features and Functionality**	**Example Uses**
Guides to Education Chats	An edchat is an online discussion on a social media platform such as X, organized around a central topic which is represented by a hashtag. Educators and leaders can engage in professional discussions, with all posts connected and threaded via the hashtag. The following are examples of resources for anyone trying to organize an edchat. • An Introduction to Education Twitter Chats (Ward, 2017) • The Complete Guide to Twitter Hashtags for Education (TeachThought, n.d.) • Office of Educational Technology Guide to Education Twitter Chats (Office of Educational Technology, n.d.) • Twitter Chats 101 (Miller, 2014)	Create a biweekly edchat using a unique hashtag such as #NorthEastOmbuds to discuss issues and problems of practice among regional peers on a shared social media platform.
Hootsuite	Hootsuite allows users to manage their social media presences from a central hub. It allows users to plan and schedule posts to several different platforms such as Facebook, X, LinkedIn, and Instagram. The tool also provides engagement analytics and offers strategic guidance.	Create and schedule a multi-platform communication campaign about a new program, and then monitor data from different platforms and at different scheduled times to determine the optimal communication strategy.
Community and Collaboration Tools		
Tools	**Features and Functionality**	**Example Uses**
Ning	Ning is an easy-to-use, low-cost hosted solution for designing, launching, and managing online communities and groups. The platform allows users with limited technical skill to set up and customize the look, feel, and features of an online community.	Build an online community with role-alike groups to allow geographically dispersed peers to collaborate via discussion boards, wikis, and content co-creation tools.
Google Sites	Google Sites allows an individual or a group of individuals without web development capabilities to build and collaborate on the development of a custom website. Sites allows developers to create a public website, a project collaboration hub, an online repository for resources, and many other types of web environments.	Quickly create a public website for a short-term project that needs to be on the web for a limited amount of time.
Social Media Groups	Social media platforms, most commonly Facebook and LinkedIn, allow users to form different types of groups for messaging, networking coordination, and communications. Groups can be public or private, and they operate with the same features and functionality as the platforms that house them.	Create a LinkedIn group for district Title I coordinators across your state to facilitate peer-to-peer networking and share ideas.

Source: United States Department of Education Office of Elementary and Secondary Education. (n.d.).

Examples of Effective Communication

As a priority school principal, one of your primary responsibilities is maintaining a safe and conducive learning environment for all students. When incidents such as fights occur, it is crucial to document them carefully and communicate the disciplinary measures taken to parents. I've outlined steps to help guide the investigation process, which can sometimes last days or weeks. Write everything down. You may forget it later.

1. **Initiate the investigation:** Once aware of a fight between students in the hallway, respond promptly. Research by Howard S. Muscott, Eric L. Mann, and Marcel R. LeBrun (2008) emphasizes the importance of addressing conflicts promptly and calmly to prevent a negative impact on the overall school climate.

2. **Gather information:** Thoroughly collect all relevant information regarding the incident. This includes identifying witnesses, reviewing any available closed-circuit television footage, and interviewing students involved. Document the time, date, location, and nature of the incident.

3. **Maintain confidentiality:** Respecting student privacy is paramount. The significance of confidentiality in maintaining trust and fostering a supportive school community cannot be underestimated. Never discuss specific details or names of students involved with anyone not directly involved in the investigation.

4. **Document the investigation:** Create a clear and concise record of the investigation. Use a standardized form or template to ensure consistency. Include details such as the parties involved, a summary of interviews conducted, any evidence collected, and statements from witnesses. Be objective and avoid personal opinions or judgments.

5. **Analyze the findings:** Review the information gathered and consider any mitigating circumstances or prior incidents involving the students. It is crucial to consider factors such as a history of bullying or conflicts that may have contributed to the incident.

6. **Determine disciplinary measures:** Based on the analysis, determine appropriate disciplinary measures. Consult your school's code of conduct and policies to ensure consistency. Consider restorative

justice practices (Muscott et al., 2008), counseling, or mediation as alternatives to suspensions or expulsions.

7. **Communicate with families:** Compose an email to parents or caregivers of the students involved, ensuring the confidentiality of other students. Begin the email by expressing your concern for student safety and emphasizing the importance of maintaining a safe learning environment. Briefly summarize the incident, mentioning that disciplinary measures have been taken. Avoid sharing sensitive details or personal opinions.

8. **Provide resources and support:** Incorporate information about available counseling services, conflict resolution programs, or other relevant resources to support the affected students and prevent future incidents. Focus on the desire for changing behaviors as the positive impact of providing additional resources to students involved in conflicts.

Here are a few key reminders.

- When in doubt, safety first.
- Ask yourself, "What is needed now?" and when you can, pause. There is a cost and consequence to every decision and nondecision.
- The *first* story is never the *only* story. Always get everyone's statement before making a decision. The first story is never the only story.

Figures 4.2 and 4.3 (page 98) provide two examples of effective communication with families and stakeholders about a change in start time and end time, including some focus on the why and research support, and checking course credits, with some emphasis on keeping families informed and providing a process to follow. Writing effective letters to your stakeholders is a necessary skill to develop, and you will have many opportunities to practice. For example, it's important to introduce yourself as the new school leader. Provide a little background on yourself, but mostly focus on your goals for the students and school. Invite parents and community to get to know you. Understand that if you are in the position of taking over midyear, there may be a lot of emotional upheaval to deal with, such as feelings of abandonment. Particularly in priority schools, high turnover in administration, sometimes midyear, can occur.

[Your Name]
Principal, [School Name]
[Date]

Dear Parents and Stakeholders,

I hope this letter finds you in good health and high spirits. As the newly appointed principal of [School Name], it is my privilege to communicate with you regarding an important matter that directly impacts the well-being and academic success of our students. I write to you today to propose a change in our school start times based on extensive research on teen brain development and the crucial need for sufficient sleep.

Adolescence is a period of rapid physical and cognitive growth, and research has shown that the sleep-wake patterns of teenagers are distinct from those of children and adults. It is widely recognized by experts, including the American Academy of Pediatrics, that teenagers require 8 to 10 hours of sleep per night to support their overall health and optimal brain development (Carskadon, 2011). Unfortunately, the current early start times in our school system often prevent students from obtaining the necessary amount of sleep, leading to a range of negative consequences.

One of the primary concerns associated with insufficient sleep is the detrimental effect on academic performance. Numerous studies have demonstrated a clear link between sleep deprivation and decreased cognitive functioning, attention deficits, and impaired memory consolidation (Dewald et al., 2010; Gruber, Cassoff, Frenette, Wiebe, & Carrier, 2012). By shifting our school start times to align with the natural sleep patterns of teenagers, we can provide an environment that fosters improved concentration, enhanced learning, and ultimately, higher academic achievement.

Moreover, sleep deprivation in adolescents has been linked to increased rates of mental health problems, including depression, anxiety, and mood disorders (Groen & Pabilonia, 2019). Adolescence is already a challenging period of life, characterized by hormonal changes and emotional upheaval. By prioritizing sufficient sleep, we can promote positive mental health outcomes and create a supportive environment for our students.

I understand that change can be met with skepticism, and I want to address some of the counterarguments that may arise. One common concern is the impact on extracurricular activities and after-school jobs. While it is true that adjusting school start times may require adjustments to schedules, research has shown that the potential benefits far outweigh any inconveniences. A study conducted by the University of Minnesota finds that schools with later start times experience reduced rates of absenteeism, tardiness, and disciplinary issues (Wahlstrom et al., 2014). This suggests that the positive effects of improved sleep on overall student well-being and academic engagement are likely to extend beyond the classroom.

In conclusion, I urge you to consider the compelling evidence concerning teen sleep needs and the potential benefits of adjusting our school start times accordingly. By prioritizing the health and well-being of our students, we can foster an environment that supports their academic success and overall development. I welcome your input and encourage you to join me in this important endeavor to enhance the lives of our students.

Thank you for your attention to this matter and for your unwavering support of our shared mission to provide the best education possible for our students.

Sincerely,
[Your Name]
Principal, [School Name]

Figure 4.2: Letter to change high school start time.

Student Transcript Credit Check

[School letterhead]

Dear Students and Parents,

We would like to inform you about the importance of regularly monitoring your student's academic progress and ensuring that they are on track to meet graduation requirements. This course credit check is designed to assist you in understanding the credit requirements for students in grades 9–12 at our public high school.

The purpose of this course credit check is to help students and parents stay informed about the number of credits required to graduate and to ensure that students are fulfilling these requirements. By regularly reviewing the credit status, students can make informed decisions about their course selections and take appropriate actions if there are any deficiencies.

Course Credit Requirements:

To graduate from our high school, students are required to earn a certain number of credits across various subject areas. The credit requirements for each grade level are as follows.

- Grade 9: 5 credits
- Grade 10: 10 credits
- Grade 11: 15 credits
- Grade 12: 20 credits

[Add any specific course credit requirements or number of credits in each subject.]

Credits are typically earned by successfully completing courses offered at our school. Each course is assigned a specific credit value, which is typically determined by the number of instructional hours. It is important to note that not all courses carry the same credit value, so it is essential to plan your course selection accordingly.

Using the Course Credit Check:

To conduct or participate in a course credit check with the assigned counselor, please follow these steps.

1. Make an appointment with the student's assigned counselor.
2. Obtain a copy of your student's transcript from the school's counseling office.
3. Review the transcript with the counselor to identify the number of credits your student has earned in each grade level and answer questions regarding options for credit recovery, if needed.
4. Calculate the total number of credits earned by your student to date.
5. Compare the total number of credits earned against the credit requirements for each grade level.
6. Identify any credit deficiencies or surpluses and make arrangements for appropriate actions.

Taking Action:

If your student has credit deficiencies, it is crucial to address them promptly. You may consider the following actions:

1. Consult with your student's counselor or academic advisor to discuss potential solutions and create an academic plan.
2. Explore opportunities for credit recovery, such as summer school, online courses, or credit retrieval programs.
3. Adjust your student's course schedule to accommodate additional courses or credit-earning opportunities.
4. Encourage your student to seek academic support from teachers, tutors, or peer study groups.

Regularly monitoring your student's course credits is essential to ensure they are on track for graduation. By conducting a course credit check, you can identify any credit deficiencies and take appropriate actions to address them. We encourage you to remain proactive in supporting your student's academic journey and to utilize the resources available at our school to ensure their success.

If you have any questions or require further assistance, please do not hesitate to contact the school's counseling office.

Sincerely,
[Your Name, Title]
[School Name]

Figure 4.3: Credit check letter template.

Both example letters give critical information: changing start and end schedules or conducting a credit check and the graduation implications. Have someone review the letters and ensure that all the important details are covered. For the review of the second letter, I suggest your lead counselor. In the case of credits and graduation or scholarship requirements, communicate in writing early and regularly. Any type of major change to families, students, or staff will take time to process, and the more information you can give, the better people can plan for change.

Conclusion

For principals in priority schools, especially if you're new to the role, making yourself a part of the school and local community is of utmost importance. The community support you can gain by being a visible and approachable leader will heavily impact your work in positive ways. The explosion of online options for communication has made visibility and communication easier than ever before, while also introducing unexpected challenges to navigate. Keep your processes for communication as simple and straightforward as possible using tools like flowcharts. Be sure to keep all your stakeholders informed in advance if changes will occur and the reasons for these process changes.

Chapter 5

Time Management and Prioritization

Efficient time management is a crucial skill for any principal, particularly for those new to their role as a priority school principal. Effective time management positively impacts educational leaders' ability to meet the diverse demands of their position, and principals in low-performing schools perceive their jobs as constantly being reactionary due to feeling overwhelmed by the diverse tasks on their plates: student discipline, organizational management, low-quality instructional practices, school event supervision, and demands from central administration, such as reporting requirements (Grissom, Loeb, & Mitani, 2015). By planning and delegating for the strengths of all individuals on the guiding coalition, as well as teacher teams, principals can shift their focus to maximize their time by engaging in proactive activities that enhance student achievement and promote a positive school climate. By effectively managing their time and prioritizing urgent tasks, priority school principals can create a positive and productive learning environment.

One approach to time management is structured planning. Research by Robert J. Marzano, Timothy Waters, and Brian A. McNulty (2005) finds that principals who engage in structured planning are more likely to allocate time for essential tasks, such as instructional leadership and teacher supervision. By prioritizing these responsibilities, priority school principals can promote a culture of continuous improvement to positively impact student outcomes by creating opportunities to engage with students, teachers, and families. This chapter discusses the challenges of prioritizing urgent tasks and ways for priority schools to get organized.

Urgent Tasks

As a new priority school principal, it is vital to identify and prioritize urgent tasks that directly impact student and staff well-being. For instance, attending to student disciplinary issues promptly fosters a safe and supportive learning environment. However, a time inventory used by principals to collect data indicates that many issues have to be prioritized in terms of student discipline when mandatory meetings or reports are coming due (Grissom et al., 2015). Use the principal time log in figure 5.1 to help you identify challenges in time management and set goals, such as a certain number of hours per week for observing instruction. This is similar to an inventory to keep track of how many hours each day you spend on teacher conferences, parent conferences, student discipline, classroom observations, supervisory duty, responding to emails, and so on. Reflecting on these data is immensely helpful to understand your focus.

Category	Day 1	Day 2	Day 3
Daily focus	Spending most of my time in classrooms and with collaborative teams	Increasing time in classrooms and with collaborative teams	Increasing time in classrooms and with collaborative teams
Classroom observations	Ninety minutes total (three classrooms)	Sixty-five minutes total (two classrooms)	Twenty minutes total (one classroom)
Student discipline	Seventy-five minutes total (three referrals)	One hundred minutes total (one serious infraction, two referrals)	Sixty minutes total (four afternoon calls to parents)
Duties (hall, lunchroom, bus yard supervision, and so on)	Bus a.m. Passing periods Three lunch periods Car pickup line after school	Bus a.m. Passing periods Three lunch periods Bus p.m.	Bus a.m. Three lunch periods Bus p.m.
Emails and office work	Two hours	Two hours	

Collaborative team meetings	Thirty minutes, department chairs	Thirty minutes, drop in	
Community engagement	Before and after school in the parking lot	Before and after school in the parking lot	
Human resources	Sixty minutes via email		Thirty minutes via email
Other			Administrative meeting at district office (six hours)

Source: Adapted from Power, 2021; Spiller & Power, 2019.
Figure 5.1: Principal time log.

Visit **go.SolutionTree.com/priorityschools** *for a free reproducible version of this figure.*

Additionally, prioritizing urgent tasks, such as providing timely feedback to teachers, enhances professional growth and student learning. *Acceleration for All* (Kramer & Schuhl, 2023) features a feedback tool to show artifacts of collaborative work both in collaborative teams and in classroom observations. It is a quick but concise checklist to note and acknowledge what the principal observed (see figure 5.2).

Classroom
- ☐ Student learning targets posted, relevant, and referred to by students
- ☐ Observable classroom routines, procedures, rituals, and smooth transitions (agenda or schedule)
- ☐ Classroom is clean, organized, and inviting
- ☐ Anchor charts to support learning are co-created, posted, and relevant
- ☐ Seating arrangement conducive to student-led and cooperative learning
- ☐ Unit and lesson plans posted outside the door

Teacher
- ☐ Effectively utilizes high-quality instructional materials
- ☐ Provides grade-level or standards-based Tier 1 instruction
- ☐ Uses gradual release model
    - ☐ I do
    - ☐ We do
    - ☐ You do in pairs
    - ☐ You do independently
- ☐ Sets goals in relation to the learning targets before, during, and after instruction to monitor student learning
- ☐ Monitors student learning (while walking around the classroom) and gives feedback to students
- ☐ Effectively uses high-impact teaching strategies to promote equity and increase engagement

Source: © 2022 Anna Strong Learning Academy. Adapted with permission; Kramer & Schuhl, 2023.
Figure 5.2: Core instructional practices walkthrough tool.

continued →

☐ Uses varied questioning (DOK levels 1–4)
☐ Uses differentiated instruction by working with small groups
☐ Utilizes instructional time effectively (bell to bell)
☐ Closes the lesson by having students reflect on the learning targets (exit ticket or formative assessment)

Students
☐ Verbalize what they are learning (aligned to learning target)
☐ Actively engage in learning
  ☐ Participate in discussions
  ☐ Work in small groups and learn from peers (collaborative learning)
  ☐ Respond to teacher instructions
  ☐ Listen or take notes
  ☐ Present or perform
  ☐ Take a test or quiz
  ☐ Read or write independently
  ☐ Answer questions
  ☐ Work on hands-on activity (such as graphic organizer or manipulatives)
  ☐ Use technology appropriately for learning task

By ensuring that feedback is given promptly, principals can support ongoing professional learning and promote instructional best practices. The list in figure 5.3 can help keep track of the most urgent tasks.

Urgent
- Student safety
  - Review and update school safety plans.
  - Conduct drills and trainings on fire safety, lockdown procedures, and active shooter response.
  - Monitor bullying and harassment incidents.
  - Investigate and respond to reports of child abuse and neglect.
- Student health
  - Ensure that all students have up-to-date immunizations.
  - Provide health screenings and referrals as needed.
  - Work with the school nurse to develop a plan for managing chronic health conditions.
- School climate
  - Create a positive and inclusive school environment.
  - Address issues of discrimination and bias.
  - Promote student engagement and participation.

Important

- Instructional leadership
    - Develop and implement a school improvement plan.
    - Monitor student achievement data.
    - Provide professional development for teachers.
    - Collaborate with teachers to create effective lesson plans.
- Staff development
    - Provide opportunities for staff to learn new skills and knowledge.
    - Create a culture of continuous improvement.
    - Support staff in their professional growth.
- Parent engagement
    - Communicate regularly with parents and guardians.
    - Build partnerships with families.
    - Involve parents in school activities.

Managerial and operational tasks

- Budget management
    - Develop and manage the school budget.
    - Track expenses and revenues.
    - Identify areas where budget cuts can be made.
- Facility management
    - Maintain the school building and grounds.
    - Make repairs and improvements as needed.
    - Ensure that the school is safe and secure.
- Human resources
    - Hire and manage staff.
    - Provide staff with benefits and support.
    - Resolve personnel issues.

Notes

- This is just a sample checklist, and the specific tasks that need to be prioritized will vary depending on the individual school and its needs.
- Principals should use their discretion to determine the urgency and importance of each task.
- It is important to regularly review the checklist and adjust the priorities as needed.

Figure 5.3: Priority school principal task prioritization list.

*Visit **go.SolutionTree.com/priorityschools** for a free reproducible version of this figure.*

The following principal checklist (figure 5.4) is intended to guide a principal with reminders for important events and benchmarks to begin the school year. This list is not comprehensive but focuses on building trust. It also allows for scheduled opportunities to get feedback from stakeholders.

Establish Relationships		
Description	Due by	Done
Send welcome letter to all families and staff (include appropriate translations for multilingual families). • Have dates established for listening tour. • Include invite in the letter with link for signup.		
Meet with outgoing principal. • Log onto various websites to change you to the principal and get the proper access codes to any reporting accounts that you will need access to.		
Meet with assistant principal. • Review district discipline policies and procedures so you know expectations (both written and unwritten). • When does the superintendent want to be notified of situations (if ever)?		
Meet with administrative assistant.		
Invite all staff members to one-to-one meetings. • Have them identify their roles, strengths, and challenges.		
Meet with building network representatives and president.		
Meet with superintendent to outline expectations.		
Host one-on-one meet-and-greet with departments and teams (clerical, leadership, content areas, and so on)		
Host a meet-the-principal event for parents.		
Connect with students and families who are new to the building and district. • What is the current practice for helping new students assimilate?		
Host a student advisory meeting (include recommended students, student council, and under-the-radar students).		
Attend PTO meeting.		
Be present at student assemblies on first day or classroom visits.		
Make a guest appearance on morning announcements (if applicable).		
Be visible and interact with students and families during morning drop-off and afternoon dismissal.		
Update school website with a personalized welcome.		
Host Coffee With the Principal periodically.		
Begin daily classroom visits.		
Attend department and committee meetings.		

Description	Due by	Done
Meet with district guiding coalition to discuss systems, processes, goals, and alignment.		
Meet with building crisis team; if one does not exist, create one.		
Walk the building with the head custodian to ensure that you have all necessary keys and access cards.		
Tour and become familiar with district facilities.		
Meet with head of food service prior to the first day of school. • How do the lunch lines work, what are the expectations for students in the cafeteria? • Who monitors the cafeteria? • What is the procedure for students who come to school with no lunch money?		
Get familiar with social media and other parent communication avenues. • How does the principal currently communicate with parents? Is there a listserv? If so, make sure you become the administrator of that account. • Make sure you are the administrator of the social media accounts. If they do not have any of these set up, get them set up and determine who will be able to post to them and what district policy there may be in terms of social media.		
Do Your Homework		
Description	**Due by**	**Done**
Review and work on mission and vision to guide tasks.		
Review crisis plan for understanding; if one doesn't exist, create it.		
Explore available school district resources.		
Review special education protocol and systems.		
Learn about school board members.		
Secure a mentor.		
Find out who orders all the supplies for the building for staff and for students. • Make sure that everything needed for the opening of school has been ordered and will be accessible.		
Review district and building safety plans and policies.		
Make note of all emergency drill plans and schedule all required drills with the head custodian and fire department.		
Review students' individual healthcare plans; you need to know who requires special care (such as severe asthma, allergies, seizures, and so on) and get any training needed to administer the medications they require in an emergency.		
Review all school board policies to make sure that you are compliant (they are different in every district).		
Review the contracts for all the networks in your building. This is where you will find their hours, required breaks, what you can and can't ask them to do, and so on. Make sure you know these things to avoid accidental grievances.		

Source: Michigan Association of Secondary School Principals, 2019. Used with permission.
Figure 5.4: Principal's checklist—ninety-day plan.

continued →

Description	Due by	Done
Review bus procedures and routes and learn the traffic pattern in your parking lot; there is always some degree of chaos during dismissal the first week. • Where is the bus loop? • Where is the student drop-off? • Are these areas well marked? • What staff members are outside before and after? Where has the principal typically been?		
Determine what observation and evaluation system is in use and seek training if needed.		
Review the previous observations and evaluations of all staff prior to starting classroom visits.		
Review current school improvement plan as well as district and building goals to ensure alignment prior to meeting with school improvement team.		

Assess the School's Current State		
Description	**Due by**	**Done**
Review historical performance data for the past three years. Identify student performance and growth trends. • Total school • Subgroups • Grade levels • Individual students (identify bottom 30 percent) Discipline • Restorative practices • Identify under-the-radar students. • Review behavioral intervention system. • Identify perception data. • Review the school improvement plan. Staff evaluations • Identify probationary and tenured staff, as well as those on individual development plans.		
Meet with outgoing administrator and current assistant principal. • Discuss findings. • Become familiarized with past, current, and future initiatives, systems, and processes. • Prepare a plan for the beginning of the year (professional learning and first three days). Conduct a building walkthrough. • Identify safety, maintenance, and custodial priorities necessary before school starts. • Review schedule and staffing (teacher certifications, experience, and placement).		

Description	Due by	Done
Conduct survey analysis with stakeholders and groups (guiding coalition, teachers, counselors, students, parent groups, and so on). <ul><li>Become familiar with past, current, and future initiatives, programs, systems, and processes.</li><li>Identify what is already working that you need to build on.</li><li>Identify barriers you need to overcome to reach goals.</li><li>Discuss results of the survey.</li></ul>		
Conduct beginning-of-the-year classroom walkthroughs.		
Assess current finances and budget (current expenditures, priorities, and annual budget process).		
Communicate goals, expectations, hopes, and plans for the least amount of disruption and continuous improvement.		

Execute Action Plan		
Description	**Due by**	**Done**
School culture and climate <ul><li>Become familiar with and understand vision and mission.</li><li>Identify the needs of the staff, students, parents, and community that need to be addressed.</li><li>Prioritize those needs.</li></ul>		
School improvement plan <ul><li>Ensure practices in place support the school improvement plan.</li><li>Identify practices that are in place that require development.</li><li>Design differentiated and staff-led professional learning around needs (instruction, assessment, and behavior).</li></ul>		
Instruction <ul><li>Identify instructional strategies that are working.</li><li>Identify instructional strategies that are missing.</li><li>Identify staff who need support.</li></ul>		
Behavior <ul><li>Identify approaches that are proactive versus reactive.</li><li>Identify students who need support (under-the-radar students).</li><li>Identify staff who need support with classroom management.</li><li>Provide opportunities for support.</li></ul>		
Maintenance and operations <ul><li>Ensure building safety.</li><li>Identify staff and building needs.</li><li>Monitor cleanliness.</li></ul>		

A reproducible for a monthly principal's calendar to personalize your needs throughout the year can be found in the appendix (page 169).

Organization

With a to-do list that is never completed, constant emails to respond to, and unexpected emergencies, it can be challenging to stay on top of everything as a priority school leader. However, parents and staff take note of a leader whose office is chaotic and disorganized. By planning and implementing a filing system, priority school leaders can manage their daily tasks and also proactively plan. Being organized helps to supervise student events and stay connected to their purpose. I have had records requested up to three years after an incident or event. Organized files can save you or your successor hours, or even days, of time.

Assess Your Needs

Before establishing a filing system, it is crucial to assess your specific needs as a school leader. Consider the types of tasks you regularly encounter, the frequency of emergencies, and the volume of emails you receive. This self-assessment will help determine the structure and flexibility required when organizing your filing systems.

Determine Priorities

Once you have assessed your needs, it is important to identify your priorities. Categorize your tasks into different levels of urgency and importance. For example, I use a regular tray for routine daily tasks and a red tray for high-priority issues. This categorization will guide you in allocating your time and resources effectively. Consider using a color-coded system or creating a priority matrix to visually represent your priorities. A system called the future file, drawn from Justin Baeder's Principal Center (www.principalcenter.com) is a particularly useful option (see pages 112–113).

Establish a Physical or Digital Filing System

Whether you prefer a physical or digital system, ensure that it is easily accessible and well-organized. If using a physical system, consider using labeled folders, binders, or file cabinets. For digital systems, create well-structured folders on your computer or cloud storage platform.

Develop a Daily Routine

Allocating specific time slots for different tasks, including reviewing and completing tasks from your filing system, is an important part of staying organized. These may seem like common sense, but the volume of correspondence, documentation, and tasks to be completed can quickly become overwhelming—especially in a priority school where there are likely more accountability measures. This routine should also include time for email communication and responses. By dedicating specific time to these activities, you can avoid distractions and stay focused on your priorities. I advise leadership teams to block off an hour daily to review and respond to emails. In that timeframe, a priority school principal can categorize and prioritize what is most urgent.

Stay Agile for Emergencies

Despite careful planning, emergencies can and will arise unexpectedly. As a priority school leader, it is crucial to be agile and able to pivot when necessary. Build flexibility into your organization system by keeping an *emergency* or *urgent tasks* folder. Regularly review this folder and adjust your priorities accordingly. By proactively managing emergencies within your system, you can minimize disruptions and maintain overall organization.

Creating and adhering to an organization system is crucial for priority school leaders to effectively manage their tasks, plan student events, and respond to emergencies. By assessing needs, determining priorities, establishing a filing system, developing a daily routine, and staying agile, school leaders can enhance their organizational skills and excel in their roles. With consistency, this system will undoubtedly contribute to more efficiency and less reactive actions. Lastly, unannounced visitors will see a leader who has everything under control when they come to your office unexpectedly.

Conclusion

Staying organized is critical to the success of any leader; however, in the case of a priority school principal, your days rarely look the same. Staying organized often depends on others who impact your day: teachers, students, administrators, family members, and district employees. Often, their needs supersede your scheduling efforts, and you're quickly required to make adjustments to your intended tasks. The tools in this chapter are intended to use proven means from the field to help you stay on top of the ever-growing tasks, documents, meetings, and appointments under your umbrella.

HOW TO KEEP YOUR DESK CLEAR WITH THE FUTURE FILE

Future File Setup

The future file system has been in use for generations. You'll be amazed at its elegant effectiveness in keeping your desk clutter-free. Here's how to set it up.

The future file is simply a set of forty-three folders.

- Twelve folders for the months of the year, January through December
- Thirty-one folders for the days of the month, one through thirty-one

The system works on a rolling basis, so you never need more folders, and you always have thirty-one days of daily folders and twelve months of monthly folders in which you can "snooze" any document—or really, any flat object that will fit into a file folder, such as a CD or flash drive. See figure 5.5 for a visual.

Create Your Folders

I recommend using normal letter-sized manila folders, but if you want to get fancy, heavier folders are fine, too.

Label the folders 1 through 31 and January through December. I recommend using a label maker or Avery 5160 file folder labels—the better your system looks, the more likely you are to take pride in using it.

Have an administrative assistant make you a set as well as a set for the office staff if you'd like.

Organize the Folders

Arrange the folders in the following order, from front to back (let's assume today is July 15).

- Tomorrow's folder (for example, 16 for the 16th of the current month)
- The rest of the days for the current month (for example, 17–31)
- Next month's folder (for example, August)
- The remaining daily folders, in order (1–15), representing those days next month (for example, August)
- The rest of the months (for example, September–June), allowing you to snooze documents for up to a year

Each morning, you'll find the folder for that day at the front of the set. If today is the 15th of the month, tomorrow you'll see the 16 folder at the front, followed by 17, 18, and so on, up to 31. You'll then see the new month's folder, followed by the rest of your daily folders.

Decide Where to Keep the Future File System

You may be tempted to keep the future file system in a desk drawer or file cabinet, but at least at the beginning, I recommend keeping it in a standing file box on your desk or somewhere else where you can see it and easily reach it.

When you start snoozing documents, the greatest danger is that out of sight will be out of mind, so to avoid forgetting about the system entirely, keep it where you won't be able to miss it. Having the system handy will also reduce the difficulty of adding documents to it.

Set Reminders to Check It

In time, you'll develop the habit of checking your folder for the day each morning. At the beginning, though, you'll need to set a specific reminder to pull out the folder first thing when you arrive (or right before you leave on the previous day). You can put an appointment on your calendar or have an administrative assistant be responsible for reviewing the future file with you each morning.

Whatever you do, don't allow a day to go by without checking the system. Even if it's empty, developing the habit and trusting the system are essential to using the system effectively.

Check and Move Today's Folder

When you check your daily folder:

- Remove everything from it and place it in your inbox
- Move the folder so it represents the same day in the following month (for example, if it's the 15th, move it behind the 14 folder to represent the 15th of next month).
- If there are fewer than 31 days in the month, such as February or April, check the remaining daily folders on the last day of the month.

If it's the first of the month, you'll also need to check the monthly folder and put each item in your inbox or a daily folder.

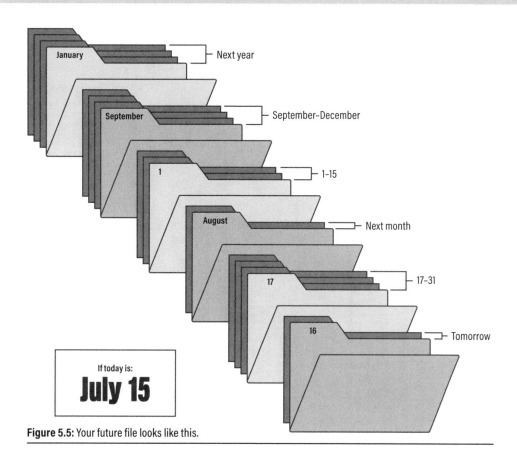

Figure 5.5: Your future file looks like this.

Do the Work

Once the day's documents are on your desk, commit to either dealing with them that day or planning a specific day in the future—with time set aside on your calendar—so the future file doesn't become a tool for procrastination.

Use Complementary Tools

The future file works best in concert with other tools, including your to-do list and your calendar.

Source: Principal Center, n.d. Adapted with permission.

When you snooze a document, add whatever work it represents to your to-do list, where you can concisely review it alongside your other pending tasks and projects.

And if a document will take a while to deal with, make sure you make an appointment on your calendar to block off time to work on it. Don't do this for minor items. Be realistic—if it's going to take twenty or thirty minutes, that time isn't going to be available unless you block it off.

Chapter 6

Delegation and Monitoring

Delegation requires trust. Relinquishing control, although difficult for many school leaders, is essential to building shared ownership and a culture focused on teamwork. The pressure for priority school leaders to fix what is broken is immense and can create a need to try and tackle everything at once, which makes it unlikely to do everything well. Assistant principals and other teacher leaders or support staff should also be a part of the solution. Assistants, after all, are there to assist the leader. Most people, in my experience, want to be a part of the solution, not just perpetuate the problem. A priority school principal can exponentially increase their reach by sharing their expectations with the guiding coalition and delegating to help alleviate the workload and also empower and grow more leaders. Trust grows when your team knows you value their contributions toward the school's mission and vision. Conversely, a priority school leader who does not delegate important work or ask for updates sends the message that no one else is capable.

There are mutual benefits to delegating and monitoring rather than trying to do it all oneself. Especially in times of volatility and uncertainty, anxiety can insidiously impact a school's culture. According to researcher John Hagel III (2021), "It's well established in the psychology field that coming together with others can reduce anxiety—that's the idea behind group therapy." Principals must counteract subversive feelings like anxiety by building a spirit of collegial support. The collaborative foundation of PLCs is based on sharing best practices, having a common focus on student learning, and providing support for both new and veteran colleagues. Asking for the guiding coalition to bring updates and discuss what they are observing is key to moving a priority school forward.

Delegation doesn't mean a lack of accountability. Priority school principals need systems for monitoring the work of teams within the school that are effective but not smothering. This ensures the school is doing what it needs to do and builds capacity: "Monitoring—measuring, observing, and reviewing work—is essential for promoting strong employee and organizational performance" (Melena, 2018). This chapter covers loose and tight leadership, accountability, and the notion of cross-training as a way to share responsibilities and ensure the seamless running of the school.

Loose and Tight Leadership

Focusing on what matters means a principal is selectively strategic in the *non-negotiables*. In *Learning by Doing*, DuFour and his colleagues (2024) discuss how a balance of simultaneous *loose and tight* structures creates both accountability for the non-negotiables as stated by the principal and also autonomy for the teachers as to *how* they will instruct students in the guaranteed and viable curriculum. For example, a principal might decide that non-negotiables in the school include using data to drive growth in learning for every student, being prepared for classroom instruction and collaborative meetings, and adhering to the approved curriculum and pacing. What matters most should be student learning, especially in the context of priority schools, where, by definition, there is a gap between where students ought to be and where they currently are in achieving mastery.

Establishing structures and processes in which stakeholders know what is loose and what is tight can help empower the guiding coalition by giving them the autonomy to get results in their own way rather than micromanaging all the steps to reach the outcomes. See figures 6.1, 6.2 (page 118), and 6.3 (page 119). Teachers need to understand what the principal expects as non-negotiables and what areas are open to creative interpretation. For example, principals expect teachers to adhere to teaching the standards and keep up with the district's

Building: _____ **Principal:** _____

"To monitor loose and tight leadership, leaders must put a process in place to monitor each team's work—the products of their work (the quality of what they produce), their processes (how they do their work), and most important, the results of their work (the effects of their work on student learning). Without a process for monitoring teams, the principal will not know when a team is struggling and will be unable to fulfill their responsibility of helping each team succeed in what members are being called on to do" (DuFour et al., 2024, p. 76).

What we're tight on this school year, specific to the PLC process and the four critical questions	The products, processes, and results we commit to monitoring across the year
Teaching the state standards and focusing on the identified essential standards	Lesson plans turned in weekly for feedback
Grade-appropriate curriculum resources that have been vetted and adopted by the district	Ensuring all resources are available and up to date
Common formative assessments on the agreed-on cycle	Data input for common formative assessments in the student information system

Source: Adapted from Dougherty & Reason, 2019.
Figure 6.1: Tool to monitor loose and tight leadership.

*Visit **go.SolutionTree.com/priorityschools** for a free reproducible version of this figure.*

pacing guidance to cover the standards within instructional calendar days. There is latitude in the types of activities and connections to real life that a teacher can make to engage students in the lesson. The lesson plan template may be tight, but the chosen manipulatives are loose, with options for choice or creativity. These are useful tools to help make your expectations clear and leave no room for "we didn't know!" Clarity helps everyone understand the expectations and rise to meet them.

Individually or as a guiding coalition, reflect on each of the following questions regarding the work of PLCs. For each question:

- Cite specific examples to illustrate how loosely or tightly this item is controlled.
- Consider whether moving either way on the loose and tight continuum would improve PLC effectiveness.
- Write down action steps to take to achieve balance.

1. Do you have a professional development plan for covering topics your PLC needs? Does it cover an adequate time frame?

   Conduct classroom observations to help identify where training may be needed, survey teachers to see where they would like additional support and learning, and offer differentiated offerings.

2. Do you have procedures for evaluating whether the professional development is resulting in classroom changes or improvements in student achievement?

   Conduct surveys to get feedback on the value of professional learning. Schedule classroom walkthroughs for data and evidence that learning is translating to classroom practices.

3. Do you regularly revise the professional development schedule based on classroom evidence or changes in teacher or student needs?

   This plan should be adaptable based on what data show is needed.

4. Are expectations clear when collaborative teams decide to implement new strategies? Do teachers agree on what those expectations mean?

   The team's minutes should be available to review for feedback. Also, frequent drop-ins give team support and guidance.

5. Is there room for innovation or differences in style as to how teachers meet those expectations?

   Share innovative and engaging lessons in the team time.

6. Have you established procedures for assessing whether students are learning what is taught?

   Common formative assessments are aligned to the essential standards and the pacing. This is monitored by instructional coaches.

7. Are teachers encouraged to seek new ways to assess student progress?

   New formative assessment practices are shared in team meetings.

8. Does your school or PLC have clear procedures for helping students who are struggling?

   Tier 3 flex time is built into the daily schedule.

9. Do you have regularly scheduled meetings?

   Paid collaborative time is built into the contractual day.

10. Is the meeting routine set, or does it vary according to needs?

    Occasionally, there are added meetings during plan time, but those are rare—like testing preparation days.

Source: Adapted from Kise & Russell, 2010.

Figure 6.2: Reflection on loose and tight PLC leadership.

*Visit **go.SolutionTree.com/priorityschools** for a free reproducible version of this figure.*

Try filling this out individually with your guiding coalition members and as a team, accompanied by discussion. For each of the following decisions, the guiding coalition should decide whether it is a loose decision (left up to the team) or a tight decision (left up to leaders).

Activity, Process, or Task	Loose	Tight
Question 1: What do we want our students to learn?		
Who will determine the power or priority standards—each school or a team of representatives for the entire district?		
Which subject or grade-level standards will be done first, next, and so on?		
Who will decide the completion date for power or essential standards?		
Who will determine when and how the vertical alignment process for power or essential standards will occur?		
Who will decide the pacing for the power or essential standards?		
Who will make specific curricular decisions (textbooks, instructional strategies, and so on)?		
Question 2: How will we know if our students are learning?		
How frequently will teams use common formative assessments?		
Who will write the common formative assessments?		
Will we use technology to score common formative assessments?		
Will we use technology to warehouse data from common formative assessments?		
What, if any, interim or benchmark assessments are used?		
Question 3: How will we respond when some students don't learn?		
How will we provide time for each tier of response?		
Who will provide each tier of response?		
What universal screener and progress-monitoring tools will be used to identify students?		
How will students be moved between tiers?		
What data will be kept on students for providing RTI?		
Question 4: How will we extend and enrich the learning for students who are already proficient?		
Who will provide response for these students?		
How will the results be reported?		
How will students be identified for each tier?		

Source: © 2014 by Kim Bailey, Chris Jakicic, & Jeanne Spiller. Used with permission.
Figure 6.3: Loose versus tight decisions.

*Visit **go.SolutionTree.com/priorityschools** for a free reproducible version of this figure.*

Guiding Coalition Meetings

Some of the leadership discussions around what is loose and what is tight in a school must happen with the guiding coalition or leadership team. Some priority school leaders may have to work with an existing leadership team because staff may have inherited or are contractually bound for a year, depending on the state and district. In all cases, a priority school leader must help build the capacity of the team members to ensure that the work is moving forward and to help monitor that work in the collaborative teams. The artifacts of learning will show if the work is being done with fidelity.

Whether meetings are structured weekly meetings or daily huddles, a regularly scheduled check-in time is necessary for feedback and the opportunity to correct, clarify, or redirect. Project management applications like Monday.com and Asana (www.asana.com) are efficient ways to track workflow but can quickly become another place that your guiding coalition needs to add time to their workday. I find that while they aren't always sustainable in a school setting, they can be more effective in central office departments or larger projects. It takes training and habitual use of the program to ensure that it is updated—having a person who manages these platforms is ideal. Use team meetings and one-on-one time for task management and clarification of roles and responsibilities. The division of roles and responsibilities template from chapter 2 (figure 2.2, page 52) was created in the field; priority school leaders can share it in a folder where the team can access it to input and track tasks.

Feedback and Management

Critical feedback is necessary for organizational growth overall, and that can only be cultivated within a culture of continual dialogue about what you and your team members are doing well and what needs improvement. *Harvard Business Review* offers copious research and many articles focused on developing flexible and responsive leadership: "Soliciting clear, actionable feedback allows you to make better, more informed decisions and pivot when necessary" (Scott, Fosslien, & Duffy, 2023). All leaders need to have honest and transparent input on how well their employees are seeing responsiveness, job efficacy, and overall value in their positions.

What I often experienced and observed in schools is that when things are going smoothly, people have the patience and time to follow established school structures; however, when things are chaotic, people tend to react emotionally or spontaneously and often go around the process to accomplish the end goal.

As challenging as it may be to allow for the process or system to work, a leader must show faith in the process and hold others accountable. Annual review of processes allows for improvement or refining unnecessary steps, so if a process is ignored altogether, it usually is not seen as valuable, or there is a lack of understanding of the need for the steps. Be willing and able to share the why. As a priority school principal, I started to incorporate a process review that began with a survey to ask what processes are not serving staff or student needs. I asked for input that I could take to the leadership team, along with possible solutions.

For example, through a process review, you might receive feedback that your hiring process is confusing or is not working well enough. This lets you know to add a line item to an upcoming guiding coalition meeting about auditing the current hiring process. If your school has a faculty advisory committee, this is a great way to get their input and feedback on possible revisions of current systems and also the creation of new procedures that may be needed. Another example would be a process for students to schedule time with a counselor that allows them to express the level of urgency they feel. Some students wait months for an appointment, and by that time, they may no longer be able to address the need, or a deadline has passed. This is especially the case in large high schools that are also priority schools.

Unfortunately, there are times when a leader must address issues in more formal ways once a teacher or staff member has had the opportunity to change and improve practices. Those types of critical conversations may lead to a growth plan (see chapter 4, page 87). But first, the plan for support and continual dialogue should be part of the way business is done—often, this can feel like micromanagement to some employees. Therefore, seek to provide clarity in roles, delegation, and overall tasks. There are various ways you can delineate and clarify lanes for employees. A study by Jack Zenger and Joseph Folkman (2014) finds that people overwhelmingly feel that corrective feedback helps improve performance.

Accountability

With guiding coalitions or leadership teams, reciprocal accountability can be a means to have checks and balances in an organization. Accountability holds us to our word and ensures a higher rate of effective follow-through. Sylvia Melena (2018) presents three pillars of strong supervisor-employee relationships in her book *Supportive Accountability: How to Inspire People and Improve Performance*: (1) trust, (2) effective communication, and (3) empowerment. While I discuss communication in chapter 5 in relationship to visibility (see page 101), in this chapter, I dive deeper into trust and empowerment.

Relationships and Trust

Leaders can build trust through consistency, follow-through on commitments, credibility, and integrity. When your team members understand the why behind your decisions and feel that you uphold that why in challenging moments, trust grows. Everyone in an organization contributes to building two-way trust as a transaction. Covey (2018) cites "appropriate levels of trust with co-workers" that are based on our past shared experiences and the level of credibility that we have established.

Following through on commitments is a tangible way that stakeholders, including parents, staff, students, and community partners, can gauge trust in their school leaders. Interestingly, through my conversations with parents, teachers, and business partners, following through and circling back is also a notable weakness in many organizations. To be fair, I believe this is due to many variables in any given school day that lead to unpredictable schedules for principals, the wait time needed to gather information, and the ability to frame follow-up conversations with a resolution that also honors the private information of often multiple parties in any given situation.

Annually, a priority school principal or leader should engage in *stop, start, or refine* exercises to reevaluate what is working, what is not, and what needs tweaking in the organization. Credibility comes into play for most educators when they see how their leaders choose to adopt or deflect new initiatives. Collective discussions about the research needed should include who will be most affected, how the work will be dispersed, and what type of training is involved. This goes back to building trust—a leader must be willing to say *no* when there is not a compelling argument for giving more work to the faculty and staff, especially if there is no funding or committed support.

Empowerment Through Delegation

Extending what Covey (2018) calls *smart trust* also means gauging the knowledge, expertise, and willingness to learn when delegating tasks to one's team. As a priority school principal, I continually observed the same high performers taking on additional tasks and responsibilities in leadership—either for the leadership experience or as passion projects. Spread tasks among the team to maximize your collaborative efforts, enhance skills and experience, and avoid burnout to maintain sustainability. This also means asking your guiding coalition to stretch their comfort zones to meet all the needs of the school. When priority school leaders continuously seek the same handful of teacher leaders to hold up as those pushing the collaborative work forward, it can be perceived as favoritism by others who are not in that group and simultaneously burn out the most dedicated educators. Building a culture of improvement means also building up your least effective team members, which can be hard to do. Priority school leaders feel the urgency and need to build trust. They need to ensure that teams won't be overwhelmed with work just because they are passionate and skilled. In the next section, I'll explain how cross-training can help.

Cross-Training

In the dynamic environment of priority schools, priority school leaders must ensure the sustainability of services even when key personnel are absent or on extended leave. The concept of cross-training has emerged as an effective strategy to address this challenge because of how it equips all school personnel with the necessary skills and knowledge to step into different roles when needed. In doing so, cross-training promotes continuity and reliability in delivering services.

Importance of Cross-Training

Cross-training is an essential component of a sustainable and efficient priority school organization. It ensures that the absence of a single individual does not disrupt the seamless operation of school services. When personnel are cross-trained, they possess a broader skill set, enabling them to assume multiple responsibilities and maintain service standards even in the absence of specific individuals. This contributes to a more efficient and resilient school environment during flu season or in the event of family emergencies that require staff to be absent for an extended period of time.

Research Supporting Cross-Training

Several studies have demonstrated the positive impact of cross-training in various organizational settings, including schools. A study conducted by Aleksander P. J. Ellis and Matthew J. Pearsall (2011) finds that cross-training significantly reduces the negative effects of employee stress during absences, leading to increased productivity and employee satisfaction. Similarly, research by James R. Gallo and Lisa A. Steelman (2019) highlights the positive correlation between cross-training, feedback for improved performance, and employee engagement, emphasizing the benefits of a flexible and adaptable workforce.

Implementing Cross-Training in Priority Schools

To ensure effective cross-training in a priority school, leaders need to adopt a strategic and comprehensive approach. The following guidelines can help school leaders create sustainability. Understanding the responsibilities of all your team's roles and sharing that knowledge with at least one person keeps the work in motion regardless of absences or emergencies.

- **Identify critical roles:** Identify the key roles within the school that require cross-training to maintain service continuity. These may include the principal, assistant principal, administrative assistant or office manager, teachers, media specialist, counselor, support staff, and interventionist. As I discussed in chapter 2 (page 37), role clarity for each of these is important—both so that everyone knows what is expected of them and so that others know what each role entails and when they might be expected to step in.

- **Develop cross-training programs:** Create comprehensive cross-training programs tailored to each role. These programs should cover the necessary knowledge, skills, and responsibilities of the respective positions. Incorporate both theoretical and practical aspects to enhance the learning experience.

- **Establish mentorship opportunities:** Encourage experienced personnel to mentor others in their areas of expertise. This will facilitate the transfer of knowledge and build a culture of continuous learning and development. I have made this a collaborative discussion to see who is most capable and has some crossover skills to support another team member. As a rule, everyone has a buddy.

- **Regularly assess progress:** Implement regular assessments to evaluate the effectiveness of cross-training efforts. Feedback from personnel and stakeholders should be sought to identify areas for improvement and address any challenges that arise. Quarterly meetings should include a supervisor for feedback, especially after someone has been absent and their duties were picked up by the buddy. A debrief and follow-up can help evaluate the sustainability plan's effectiveness.

Cross-training is a powerful tool that enables priority school leaders to ensure the sustainability of services even in the absence of key personnel. Backed by research evidence, cross-training has been proven to increase engagement and productivity, meaning that schools can more seamlessly pursue their mission to ensure that all students learn. Embracing cross-training is a significant step toward building a resilient and sustainable school system, whether a key employee is out for a day or an extended absence.

Conclusion

Planning for a new and sustainable rollout of communication to teachers, staff, families, and other guiding coalition members can help the year begin and continue smoothly. Planning for all the team's known events and supports can help you when inevitable and unexpected events occur. Clarity will help everyone achieve the vision in your school. Take the time before the year starts to meet with your guiding coalition and hear their perspectives as you set forth to set the course for the year.

Chapter 7

Culturally Sensitive Events and Traditions

As society becomes increasingly diverse, schools are faced with the challenge of addressing culturally divisive issues that arise within their communities. In 2020, the diversity index of the total population was 61.1 percent, meaning that there was a 61.1 percent chance that two people chosen at random were from different racial or ethnic groups. In 2010, there was a 54.9 percent chance. This indicates that the diversity of the U.S. population increased between 2010 and 2020 (Rabe & Jensen, 2023). Looking closer at the 2020 census, the population aged 18 and over had a diversity index score of 58.3 percent, while the population under age 18 had a diversity index score of 68.5 percent. At the national level, the younger population is more racially and ethnically diverse than the adult population (Rabe & Jensen, 2023).

Without a doubt, the 2020s have seen political and cultural spheres overlap with K–12 education. A school leader may face issues that are more polarizing than ever, as heightened political tensions affect decisions about equity, inclusion, and tolerance from the curriculum to the historical traditions in almost every school community. School leaders once may have been able to leave racism and other issues out of their buildings, but they are not immune to real-world problems. School leaders can use incidents to start conversations that many stakeholders have been unwilling to tackle; these instances can be an on-ramp for a deeper discussion about cultural awareness in schools. Priority schools functioning as PLCs will have a powerful framework at the ready to address these difficult topics; the focus on collaboration, learning, and results means that all voices can be heard, solutions can be offered, and progress can be celebrated.

To promote a learning environment that is a place of belonging for people of varying backgrounds, it is crucial for school principals to actively engage stakeholders in open and respectful dialogue. By fostering a culture of inclusivity and promoting consensus on hard topics, principals can create an atmosphere that values diversity while nurturing the academic growth of all students. This chapter is focused on creating ways for priority school principals to hear divergent voices and take them into account when they hold discussions or make difficult decisions in a highly political climate.

Harmful Events or Incidents

Journalist Cliff Brunt (2022) documents several incidents related to high school football teams across the United States, including a video of students holding a mock "slave auction," students at a game wearing shirts spelling out a racial slur, and students at another game in blackface. Somehow, these seemingly unbelievable situations continue to happen in our schools. Emphasizing and embracing cultural diversity is something a principal can spearhead and model every day to respond to and alleviate hateful incidents such as these. When such incidents do occur, have a process in place to respond.

Importance of Cultural Diversity

Priority school principals hold a crucial role in shaping the educational environment for their students. Principals are navigating the complexities of cultural diversity in a difficult sociopolitical climate. I often see that schools mirror what's happening in society at large, which is understandable because students hear the opinions of family, media, and friends—all shaping their perspectives on what's going on around them. The ability to understand the validity of information is an imperative part of what educators must provide for their students: "Children must be taught how to think, not what to think" (Mead, 1928). The cultural division has been exacerbated by the current flood of misinformation and disinformation that is rehashed in our school rooms after their viral flashes through social media (Long, 2024). As leaders, we have an obligation to help students understand the validity and credibility of what they are reading, hearing, and seeing on the internet.

Principals must approach culturally sensitive issues with empathy and respect to respond in a thoughtful and transparent manner. In 2017, in a Phoenix school district, a senior who had donned a ceremonial feather on her cap was denied entry and not allowed to participate in the district's graduation. The district upheld the decision to restrict the student from participating in the commencement ceremonies due to a rule against decorating graduation caps, which inevitably led to the family bringing a suit against the district. The case was settled, and in 2021, a law was passed protecting the rights of students to wear graduation regalia, including the right of any citizen of a federally recognized tribe to wear traditional regalia or objects of cultural significance during graduation in Arizona (Silversmith, 2023). If we are truly supporting all students and honoring cultural diversity, a student should not have to wait years for things to be put right.

Cultural sensitivity is vital in public schools, as it acknowledges and respects the diverse backgrounds and traditions of students and their families—especially as backgrounds diversify and families blend. Research indicates that a culturally sensitive environment enhances students' overall academic performance, promotes positive social interactions, and contributes to students' emotional well-being (Banks & Banks, 2013; Farmer, 2020; Nieto, 2008; Re'vell, 2019; Sleeter, 1997).

Schools become a microcosm of greater societal biases and racism (Howarth & Andreouli, 2014). One situation I witnessed during my first year as a new principal comes to mind. Monitoring lunch duty, I heard a ninth-grade girl exclaim, "He looks like a runaway slave!" Immediately, I approached the table, where a light-skinned Black girl was pointing and laughing at an upperclassman. He looked a bit confused and unsure of what to say, with a tentative and nervous smile on his face. I asked both students to come to my office. When I asked the young lady why she made the statement, she said he was "so dark skinned." I asked her if she thought the statement was appropriate, and she responded, "I'm Black, so I can't be racist." I asked the young man how the statement made him feel, and again, he seemed to hesitate and said that all the students made fun of his dark skin. In a predominantly Black school (over 80 percent), it seemed absurd to be having this discussion, but degrees of "Blackness" is a topic that students latch onto regarding not only skin color but overall verbal communication and dialect, outward appearance, hair texture, and bone structure.

What I didn't know a lot about at the time was that colorism is a named type of bias. Teacher and writer David Knight (2015) describes *colorism*, first coined by author Alice Walker, as "within-group and between-group prejudice in favor of lighter skin." Knight (2015) discusses how implicit biases such as colorism can influence student learning, disciplinary consequences, and social interactions. One thing I was not prepared for was how to discuss colorism and implicit bias with young students. The Southern Poverty Law Center provides a toolkit at www.learningforjustice.org/magazine/fall-2015/toolkit-for-whats-colorism with guidance for classroom conversation that leaders may find useful.

If you find yourself in a similar situation, what will you do? What if the situation involves more participants? What if it's on video and goes viral?

A Process for Addressing Culturally Sensitive Incidents

Imagine students mocking undocumented immigrants by pretending to guard a "wall." Making light of the danger that undocumented immigrants face by using their circumstances for satire is not a political or ethical stance that a school should allow or take. Again, we wonder—how? But the real question that principals should answer is what to do next.

- Describe the event and what was observed if you are walking into an event or a planning session for an inappropriate event (date, time, individuals, or teams included).

- Share any video or pictures while protecting the confidentiality of students and others who may be depicted. If pictures are on social media, consider requesting that the platform remove them if they violate the rules of the platform. Use tools like blurring to protect the identities of students who are minors. Even if the social media platform shows faces, it is likely that images will already have been shared with others, but as leaders, we should set the model. You can also consider verbally describing an image or video that is overtly disturbing or offensive rather than showing it to your guiding coalition when crafting communication regarding the events. In the case of discipline associated with such an event, only sharing information with parents regarding their child is often one of the most polarizing issues a principal can face. Give all information to legal authorities, but only share what each parent should know about their child. If sharing any information gathered from the site-level investigations, using student statements, ensure that specific student names or identifiers are not shared. Sadly, in extreme situations, people seek retaliation, and the school should not add to the information that can be used to cause harm to anyone.

- Explain and connect the historical connotations, especially how something that may have once been accepted is not appropriate in honoring all voices and experiences of the students, staff, and community.

- Share a variety of perspectives, especially if statements have been made.

- Ask for possible solutions that could achieve a similar outcome (for example, school spirit or fundraising), and emphasize that a diverse committee of stakeholders could create an alternative event.

- Ask for ideas to include in an apology statement and how it might be shared with governing board members, media, and other stakeholders.

- Take appropriate time to think about the responses, share artifacts, and accept feedback. In most cases, an immediate apology is needed, along with a follow-up message of rectifying steps over the course of a week, which is a good general timeline. If a leader has the opportunity to state that discipline will follow according to the code of conduct, that may be appropriate (again, while protecting the identities of students and other minors, no names, identifying information, or the nature of the consequences should ever be made public); however, if sessions to develop alternative fundraisers or celebrations are needed, it is appropriate to say that stakeholders will be invited to engage in some discussions to brainstorm new ways to celebrate or develop updated traditions that reflect the current and future school community and the board's core values. Importantly, follow up and communicate how that will happen and the outcomes—this can take weeks or months, depending on the engagement feedback. Developing a sense of urgency and prioritizing is generally based on safety—if an issue is tied to safety, it is a priority and simultaneously urgent. If you have the option to collaborate and hear a variety of perspectives, it may still be a priority but not highly urgent.

It's important to try and remain objective and not take criticism personally. Bringing student government and parent-teacher organizations into the conversation can be time-consuming but helpful. Use networks, such as other school leaders within or outside the organization, to share templates and ideas for communication.

William M. Ferriter and Eric Twadell (Solution Tree, 2023) offer suggestions for using artificial intelligence (AI) to generate items to support consistency in communication, such as school letter templates. An AI assistant could also take notes or create transcripts of meetings. When a difficult or sensitive issue arises, having a way to draft communication and phrasing about it can be immeasurably helpful. Using AI to craft a few potential versions of a letter to parents and staff is a great way to have a review of your thoughts. I would recommend having the draft reviewed by an administrator to help you fill in missed information and craft the tone appropriately.

Outdated Traditions

A school's traditions signal what the school community values and accepts. In school communities where the leader hasn't grown up or lived in the neighborhood for long, it can be difficult to understand the importance of ritualized traditions. So, what's the best way to know what is positive, inclusive, and equitable and what needs to be eradicated? Forming committees that include teachers, parents, students, and other community stakeholders can help bring perspective to issues that may seem like common sense to a new leader in a priority school.

These committees can review traditional events and discuss possible barriers for various groups, including those with unique physical limitations, food allergies, and cultural sensitivities. The committee should understand that its role is to review and update traditional events to reflect changing demographics and cultural awareness. As a team working within a PLC, such committees should set norms for their decision making, have goals for inclusion and equity, evaluate data, and report on their work to remain transparent. The collaborative structures of the PLC process can help guide a team to use the power of more than one perspective and multiple skill sets and backgrounds.

School spirit weeks and homecoming events are times when many school communities look forward to traditions. My own student council reviewed some of the roles associated with homecoming and decided that the titles of *king* and *queen* were not inclusive of all students. They decided to add *royalty* to the categories so that all students could be included, regardless of gender. There can be other more operational traditions, such as academic or curriculum nights, STEM events, and program showcases that might be traditional in your community. Looking at ways to update cultural practices and traditions allows students and teachers to engage in a positive way. Having your committee evaluate plans for celebrations, showcases, and school events can help you anticipate any issues that violate your organization's values.

Strategies for principals include the following.

- **Cultivate a deep understanding:** Principals can proactively educate themselves and their staff about various cultural practices and traditions within their student population by creating opportunities for conversations and planning. For example, as a principal, I had a student advisory committee, which I continue to engage with in my newer role as a superintendent in another district. In both contexts, I included students with a variety of perspectives—some new to the school or district and others who had been in the community since preschool. Some are athletes, some are into art or STEM, and a few claimed to have nothing that interested them at school.

- **Engage stakeholders:** To effectively address culturally sensitive traditions, principals should involve all stakeholders, including students, families, teachers, and community members. Open dialogue and active listening can help principals gain insight into the perspectives of different groups and facilitate collaborative decision making. Bringing in student groups and parent or caregiver groups can help relieve the pressure of making decisions in isolation, but be prepared with norms for collaborative and respectful discussions. I found that many students living with extended family or in foster care felt they were excluded from most of the traditional school events that haven't adapted for increasingly diverse family configurations.

- **Prioritize equity and inclusion:** Like academic opportunities and extracurricular programs, principals must prioritize equity and inclusion when evaluating school traditions. Traditions can perpetuate stereotypes or marginalize certain cultural groups. For example, traditional calendar holidays in the United States do not account for all the other holidays that may be celebrated in the homes of our students and staff (Dvorak, 2021).

- **Seek alternative solutions:** In cases where a tradition may be deemed culturally insensitive, principals should explore alternative ways to preserve the spirit of the tradition while adapting it to be more inclusive. For example, my student council's move from homecoming king and queen to general royalty court was an easy shift and promoted inclusivity for all.

- **Promote education and awareness:** Principals can create opportunities for cultural education and awareness within the school community. This can include hosting cultural festivals, inviting guest speakers from diverse backgrounds, or incorporating multicultural content into the curriculum. Such initiatives can help build empathy, reduce biases, and promote inclusivity.

Priority school principals play a pivotal role in creating an inclusive and culturally sensitive environment for their students. Create opportunities to engage with students regularly outside of discipline or celebrations to truly understand the perspective of students in any context. Principals should be aware of the historical significance of school traditions and consider having a process in place to change those that need it.

Observe and Trace Historical Significance

Because traditions can often be sentimental and nostalgic for stakeholders, principals should be mindful of the potential impact of their decisions to make changes to the cultural identity of the school community while still creating a culture of belonging for all. One of the first things I considered changing at my new school as the incoming principal was the school song. If you are a veteran school leader, you are likely shaking your head as you read this. What I heard from many students and teachers was that no one knew the school song because it was outdated and the rhythm and lyrics were not relatable. The lyrics incorporated outdated stereotypes and verbiage that were offensive to some of the audience.

When I brought up this idea to the staff and at an education foundation meeting, I was informed that it would be a career-ender by a senior community member. In fact, I was privately informed that some of the scholarship donors and benefactors would undoubtedly pull their financial support. This was a swift lesson for me—traditions and historical rituals need to be looked at carefully before voicing a decision. By asking the right people who have either been in the community or a part of the staff over a significant period of time, a new leader can avoid stepping on certain landmines. After all, most school traditions are inherited and often go unquestioned, even if some staff or students are uncomfortable with their nature.

A leader should take time to understand and address the historical significance of the tradition and how or why it came to exist in the school. This helps craft the persuasive *why* behind the decision to end it. Discussions with teachers, sponsors, families, and students will all look different, but some points to include are key.

A Process for Changing Outdated Traditions

To create your evaluator committee, consider inviting staff, administrators, family members, and students to join the team. Create a clear description of their duties and how they align with the school's vision and mission. Ensure that everyone understands the reasons and process for giving feedback and updating school traditions. Students are the best members of this committee, in my experience.

Identifying Stakeholders

Engage a diverse range of stakeholders, including students, parents, teachers, administrators, and members of the wider community. Ensure representation from different cultural, religious, racial, and ethnic backgrounds to promote a comprehensive understanding of the issues at hand.

Creating a Welcoming Environment

To establish a foundation for constructive dialogue, principals must create a welcoming environment where diverse perspectives are respected and valued. Encourage open communication by actively listening to stakeholders and acknowledging their concerns. By modeling inclusivity and demonstrating a willingness to understand different viewpoints, principals can set a positive tone for discussions. In setting the tone for principals and their administrative assistants to have a productive dialogue, I model for them what a conversation could sound like at the beginning of each day. I was surprised that these daily check-ins were not naturally occurring, so we focused on a few big things to be shared by the principal and the administration (like visiting groups from the community, events, or emergency drills) and some blocks of time during the day when the principal would be in the classroom to observe instruction.

Promoting Research-Based Approaches

Research plays a crucial role in facilitating discussions on culturally divisive issues and evaluating decision making or influencing district policy. Principals should encourage stakeholders to rely on evidence-based information and research to help inform their opinions. By providing access to reputable sources, such as scholarly articles and reports, principals can ensure that stakeholders are well-informed and equipped with accurate information. For instance, research conducted by Elizabeth N. Farley-Ripple (2012) and Kara S. Finnigan, Alan J. Daly, and Jing Che (2013) shows that engaging in discussions backed by research helps individuals and teams understand the complexities of culturally divisive issues, leading to more informed decision making and increased consensus.

Principals should foster a collaborative decision-making process that involves all stakeholders. Encourage participation from teachers, parents, students, community leaders, and representatives from marginalized groups. By including diverse voices in the discussions, principals can promote a sense of ownership and shared responsibility. From curriculum adoption to holiday celebrations in the classroom—all these discussions require people with various experiences and perspectives to be able to have discussions that lead to consensus.

Facilitating Mediation and Conflict Resolution

Culturally divisive issues often lead to disagreements and conflict. Principals should be skilled in mediation and conflict resolution techniques to maintain a respectful and productive dialogue. When conflicts arise, principals should guide stakeholders toward finding common ground, emphasizing shared values and goals. Continually focus on the common goal to keep from turning a discussion into an argument when emotions run high. Think about the ground rules you expect to present before the meeting—write down the expectations for everyone to be clear. When the common goal is stated, write it on a whiteboard or a piece of paper if the group is seated at a table. Reminding the group of the goal can help prevent people from getting into sidebar discussions or being distracted.

Implementing Consensus-Building Strategies

To reach a consensus on hard topics, principals can employ various strategies, such as brainstorming, small-group discussions, and consensus voting when the best result is a majority. Principals should encourage stakeholders to share their perspectives while seeking areas of agreement that support the common goal. Engaging stakeholders in discussions on culturally divisive issues is a challenging yet essential task for principals to build a foundation of trust and ownership in new policies and procedures that nurture inclusion and equity.

Asking Culturally Sensitive Questions About Traditions and Rituals

In our rapidly changing world, educational institutions must adapt and address cultural divisions that may arise due to outdated school traditions and rituals.

As a school principal or a new priority school principal, one of your key responsibilities is to create an inclusive environment that respects and values the diverse backgrounds of your students, staff, and community. Engaging stakeholders in open discussions, backed by research and supported by examples, can help navigate complex issues and reach consensus on hard topics. By doing so, you can foster an inclusive school community that embraces cultural diversity while transforming outdated practices.

Recognizing the Need for Change

To initiate a dialogue on culturally divisive issues, the first step is to acknowledge that certain traditions and rituals may no longer align with the evolving values and beliefs of your stakeholders. This recognition demonstrates your commitment to inclusivity and sets the stage for productive discussions. Figure 7.1 provides guidance for reviewing policies and procedures. This can be used either at the classroom level or the school level.

Use the table to list the policies and practices in your classroom or school. How do these policies send messages of hope and possibility to students? Are there ways to revise your practices to intentionally send messages of hope and efficacy?

Policy or Practice	Explicit or Implicit Message to Students	Changes to Instill Hope and Self-Efficacy
Late-work policy	You are expected to do the work even without being present for instruction.	An opportunity for instruction for missed work is available during the instructional Tier 3 time.
Tardy policy	If you are late, you might as well miss the entire class period because you won't get credit after fifteen minutes.	There are systems to make up learning that was missed. Plan to make up seat time when you are able to attend class.
Celebrations	The same students are always celebrated.	The committee has created celebrations that recognize students with a variety of interests.
Homework policy		
Grading practices or policies		
In-class discussion practices		
Handling disruptive comments or behavior		

Source: Chapman & Dimich, 2011, p. 130.
Figure 7.1: Reviewing policies and practices.

*Visit **go.SolutionTree.com/priorityschools** for a free reproducible version of this figure.*

Encouraging Open Dialogue

Create a safe and respectful space where stakeholders can openly express their perspectives, concerns, and experiences related to the traditions and rituals in question. Emphasize active listening, empathy, and understanding as important elements for productive discussions. Set the norms for productive discussion. Take time to think through your opening remarks and the outcome you are seeking. Provide stakeholders with relevant research and data that supports the need for change. Research can include studies on the impact of outdated practices on marginalized groups or the benefits of embracing inclusive traditions.

Facilitating Consensus Building

As discussions progress, aim for consensus building by focusing on shared goals and values. Encourage stakeholders to find common ground and identify compromise solutions that respect diverse perspectives. Consensus may not always mean complete agreement but rather a mutual understanding and respect for each other's viewpoints. As DuFour and his colleagues (2024) put it, you have reached a consensus when the voices of everyone in the group have been heard and the will of the group is apparent, even to those who disagree. The tool in figure 7.2 can be helpful in reaching a consensus.

Step 1: Establish Clarity

Work together to write a clear statement of the decision that you are making.

_____

_____

_____

Step 2: Identify Non-Negotiables

Ask all team members to describe the factors that matter the most to them about the decision that you are making. What characteristics would a potential solution require to earn their support?

Team Member	What Matters Most About the Decisions We Are Making?

Step 3: List Areas of Agreement

Work together to find the common ground that already exists among the various thoughts and opinions of your team members. The non-negotiables generated in step 2 will help you identify where your team members agree.

We already agree on the following core ideas related to the decision that we are trying to make.

_____

_____

_____

Step 4: Develop Two Proposed Solutions

Develop two proposed solutions for the decision that you are trying to make that take the non-negotiables of your team members and your areas of agreement into account.

Proposed Solution 1	Or	Proposed Solution 2

Step 5: Summarize Your Final Decision

After discussing the two potential solutions brainstormed in step 4, summarize your final decision. Here is what we have agreed to do.

_____

_____

_____

Source: Ferriter, 2020.
Figure 7.2: Building consensus around difficult decisions.

*Visit **go.SolutionTree.com/priorityschools** for a free reproducible version of this figure.*

Implementing Change Strategically

Once a consensus is reached, develop an action plan for implementing changes to outdated traditions and rituals. Ensure that the plan respects the opinions and concerns of all stakeholders while prioritizing inclusivity and cultural sensitivity. Acknowledge who is responsible for tasks in the implementation process, possibly inviting individuals to be part of the process and recognize their contributions. Create a timeline for the rollout and communication with students and staff. Acknowledging the team's ability to come to an agreement will create momentum for shared and collaborative decision making.

As a school principal, your role in fostering an inclusive school community is of paramount importance. As a priority school principal, the stakes can be even higher under the microscope of the school improvement category (Duke, Tucker, Salmonowicz, & Levy, 2007). By engaging stakeholders in open discussions on culturally divisive issues and utilizing research with citations to support your arguments, you can navigate through challenging topics and reach a consensus. Embracing change, promoting cultural awareness, and implementing strategic solutions will not only transform outdated practices but also create a more inclusive and harmonious educational environment for all. Together, we can build schools that celebrate diversity and prepare students for a globalized world.

Conclusion

Our purpose in educating students in a priority school includes finding ways to recognize and support students from all backgrounds and experiences to reach their potential. All the tools and examples included in this chapter help you navigate an ever-changing and complicated political and social landscape. Students need our support in analyzing, verifying, and determining their own conclusions regarding many of the critical issues of our time.

Chapter 8

Social Media

Social media has become an integral part of everyday life, especially that of tween and teenage students. It offers them countless opportunities for communication, self-expression, and connecting with others. While it can be entertaining, fulfilling, and even educational, this online world also poses various risks. Students may not yet understand the instantaneous yet lasting nature of the words and images they put out into the world, making social media a potential pitfall when it combines with the impulsivity of young people.

In 2017, I received a late-night Sunday phone call regarding a Snapchat video that depicted a student with an AR-15 making threats toward our students, staff, and school. The name on the account matched a ninth-grader in our student information system. At the time, pictures and videos on Snapchat could not be saved or retrieved, but within moments, I received a screenshot from the video from both parents and students. I contacted the police and our school resource officer to start immediate action. I alerted the district office and proceeded to make the information available to the authorities. Over several hours, we communicated with staff and families via email to explain that a threat had been made against the school. Out of an abundance of caution, we canceled all classes and activities for the next day. On social media, we also posted a message stating that a threat had been made and asking anyone with information to please come forward.

Police and a SWAT team went to the home of the alleged perpetrator en masse. I watched on the news as the darkness of night around the home was completely lit up. What didn't make sense was that this was an honor student who had never been in trouble before—not even for a dress code violation. The family and student were completely taken by surprise and traumatized by the events that occurred that early morning; it was an incident of so-called *swatting*, in which someone falsely reports a victim or otherwise causes armed law enforcement to show up at a victim's address to harass or inflict harm.

This swatting incident occurred when a student in an entirely different district created a fake account to post the video and make the victim look guilty. The fake account was eventually traced to the perpetrator's IP address. The stress for all the students, staff, families, and administrators was immeasurable; however, this was nothing in comparison to the trauma endured by the family and student being swatted—the impact was so severe that they ended up selling their home and moving to another city. It was heartbreaking to me as the school principal. And to think that anyone can do such a thing in a matter of minutes from any device, at any time, is horrifying.

One of the key takeaways this situation illustrates is that students can be both the aggressors and the victims. This makes it crucial for parents and educators to be aware of potential perils for students and the community as a whole. This chapter aims to provide guidance on how to protect students from online predators and shed light on online dangers to the school community, including threats, predatory communication, and cyberbullying. While this type of situation is not limited to priority schools in particular, it creates a high-priority emergency for any site administrator and local law enforcement. Any type of safety concern is a drop-everything-and-address kind of moment. We know that threats can originate anywhere via technology. These events stop all learning and create real panic and fear. Although the majority are found to be hoaxes, they should absolutely be addressed and investigated.

Online Threats

Schools may be the target of threats made online that might be nothing more than a threat. But they might be something more, forcing schools to take them seriously. The ease and perceived anonymity with which an internet user can make these threats makes them difficult to defend against.

Swatting

Swatting is a dangerous prank and a serious crime. This malicious act often targets online personalities, gamers, or individuals involved in disputes, endangering their lives and causing emotional distress. The consequences can be severe, and families and educators need to educate students about this potential threat. In my experience, most students don't understand the ramifications of these types of pranks. Both in classrooms and schoolwide, principals must ensure that students receive clear, factual information on the consequences, trauma, and effects of these actions through responsible use of social media. These lessons should start in elementary school and continue through high school as technology evolves. We don't know what future technology will look like, but we do know it can be used for positive and negative outcomes.

Direct Threats Against the School or Students

Principals need to share a message that we are all responsible for keeping one another safe. Letting a trusted adult know about something concerning, or even possibly concerning, can save lives. Principals must enlist students to help keep the school community safe, and that comes through education and systems with which to report issues. Principals need a clear and known emergency plan aligned with local law enforcement. Those plans should not be posted online.

Predatory Communication

The internet provides a platform for online predators to exploit unsuspecting children and teens. These individuals may use various tactics, such as grooming, manipulation, or impersonation, to establish trust and exploit vulnerable individuals. It is crucial to recognize the signs of grooming and teach students the importance of not sharing personal information or engaging in risky conversations with strangers online. All students are at risk of being manipulated by predators, and in priority schools, you may have a lot of students who are home unsupervised for extended periods of time. This makes them vulnerable to online predators, both known and unknown. Family members should be vigilant about parental controls on phones. Help them understand which applications can hide messaging that may be inappropriate. Principals can directly encourage parents to get involved and check their children's texts, direct messages, and other modes of communication. Secrecy, extended isolation online, and changes in a student's behavior can be red flags. Unfortunately, students of all backgrounds are at risk of online predators.

In the digital age, students are increasingly exposed to various online platforms and applications. Many of these apps are designed to entertain, educate, and safely connect students, but they may be exploited by unsafe people to harm others. There is also a growing concern associated with the emergence of applications disguised as child-friendly tools. These deceptive apps serve as a means for predators to communicate with minors, posing serious risks to their safety and well-being. The need for increased awareness and vigilance among teachers, school leaders, and families is great.

Hidden Danger

Familiar and often-used apps, platforms, and games that seem perfectly safe to adults may hide dangers for students. Establish open conversations with students about online dangers without creating fear. Encouraging dialogue about internet safety, the importance of privacy, and the risks of sharing personal information can empower students to recognize and avoid potential threats.

Principals can familiarize themselves with privacy settings and parental control tools and software to monitor students' online activities on school devices and encourage families to do the same on personal devices. Enabling these features limits access to personal information, controls who can interact with student accounts, and monitors students' online activity. These tools can restrict access to certain apps, track usage patterns, and provide alerts for suspicious behavior. I have personally helped families create online rules for their children with parental controls. After a student was found communicating with an adult online, we worked with the parents to research and support them in adding parental controls on all their devices and monitoring their child's online activity. We suggested some rules (online time limits, blocking social media apps, and so on), but ultimately, it is up to parents and caregivers to err on the side of caution. As school leaders, we can offer our help to them to navigate the resources.

To alleviate online dangers effectively, the entire school community must remain vigilant, educate themselves, and engage in open conversations about online safety. Schools and parents can work together to help students understand how to stay safe online. Anyone who observes suspicious activity or communication should report it immediately to law enforcement agencies, such as the local police department or the CyberTipline operated by the NCMEC (www.missingkids.org/gethelpnow/cybertipline). Principals should make sure this protocol is well known to the school community so that students, families, educators, and leaders can all take a hand in protecting themselves.

Encourage all educators within the school to establish open and nonjudgmental lines of communication with students. If students feel safe sharing their online experiences, reporting any uncomfortable situations, and seeking guidance whenever they need it, educators can help them navigate potential dangers and keep them safe. Regularly discuss the possible risks of social media and what to look out for when online. Red flags to be aware of include chats that turn into uncomfortable requests for information or pictures, attempts to meet secretly in person, vocabulary that seems unlike adolescent language, excessive praising, or attempts to isolate students.

Educate students about the importance of digital literacy. Teach them to critically evaluate online content, identify fake profiles, and understand the potential consequences of sharing personal information. With the rise of AI tools and manipulative technology, we are often unaware of the ways that fake images, audio, and information are mainstreamed. Engage students in questioning around facts and evidence and ask them to show you what they are looking at and discussing. There are some telltale cartoonish signs in AI images, but they are quickly getting more defined and realistic. The validity of information is easier to assess *if* one is researching it, but many adults are not sufficiently fact-checking (Langreo, 2024). Encourage them to think twice before accepting friend requests or engaging with unknown individuals. People they don't know may have hidden motives ranging from exploitation to spreading harmful ideology. According to Raisa Masood (2024), learning to decode misinformation online is a skill that can be taught and practiced. Masood (2024) recommends helping students ask a series of metacognitive questions about a post's motivation and credibility.

- Who made this content?
- What's their possible motivation for creating it?
- Is this an advertisement, and if so, who paid for it?

Here is a list of resources to help students validate information and debunk misinformation (Knutson, 2024).

- **FactCheck.org (www.factcheck.org):** This site features entries related to the veracity of TV ads, debates, speeches, interviews, and news releases, as well as resources for checking scientific claims.

Run by the Annenberg Public Policy Center at the University of Pennsylvania, it is nonprofit and nonpartisan.

- **PolitiFact (www.politifact.com):** This site verifies statements made by politicians and rates them based on truthfulness. It also includes relevant links. It's run by the *Tampa Bay Times*, an independent newspaper.
- **Snopes (www.snopes.com):** This site documents internet rumors.
- **OpenSecrets.org (www.opensecrets.org):** This site tracks money in politics.
- **Wayback Machine (https://archive.org):** This site is a repository of archived websites so you can see what online sources said and looked like at any point in the past.

While these resources are generally not aimed at young students, educators can provide guidance on interpreting them and helping students think critically and practice determining the truth for themselves. As students get older and spend more of their time online, these habits will protect them.

Deceptive Apps

Media is outlining more deceptive applications, designed to appear harmless and appealing to children, which have become increasingly prevalent and marketed to students (Fair, 2024). According to the Federal Trade Commission, apps that hide conversations and allow users to falsify age and gender include the following high-risk list (Fair, 2024; Mejia, 2022).

- NGL
- MeetMe
- KIK
- TikTok
- Calculator%
- Holla
- Badoo
- Scout

The Federal Trade Commission cites threats for schools and students via data insecurity and access to students at a growing pace (Fair, 2024). According to *Education Week*, one in five students will receive unwanted sexual advances online (Prothero, 2024). Lauraine Langreo (2023) writes that although 86 percent of adults are concerned about their data being exposed online, the majority don't know how their and their children's data is being used. Forty percent of students and 29 percent of teachers say they know of a deepfake depicting individuals associated with their school being shared during the 2023–2024 school year, according to the nationally representative survey of high school students, middle and high school teachers, and parents. A *deepfake* is a digitally manipulated video, photo, or audio recording created using someone's voice, likeness, or both without their permission (Langreo, 2023).

These apps often masquerade as innocent games, educational tools, or social platforms, making it difficult for adults to identify potential risks. Calculator%, for example, looks like a regular tool for calculating. However, behind their seemingly benign facade lies a sinister motive: to facilitate communication between predators and vulnerable minors. Since these types of apps come and go constantly, it's most important to know the signs of a deceptive app and ensure that parents and caregivers are checking all the apps on their children's devices. All apps that look academic or have chat or messaging capabilities should be carefully examined. Principals cannot rely on technology to block fake images and apps because it's difficult to adapt rapidly enough. We should always request the latest firewalls and update them; however, check for students bypassing the firewalls with tools like virtual private networks (VPNs). Work with your school or district information technology team to have them attend cybersecurity conferences for the latest resources.

Predatory individuals exploit these deceptive apps to establish contact with unsuspecting children. By concealing their true identity, predators gain access to personal information, manipulate minors' emotions, and gradually build trust. This insidious grooming process creates an environment ripe for exploitation, blackmail, and even physical harm.

Several high-profile cases have brought attention to the dangers associated with deceptive apps, such as a teenage girl who was found in Arizona after being lured to meet a man she met playing a game on her Nintendo Switch. Law enforcement used the game to track her location and rescue her (Blasius, 2023). According to the National Center for Missing and Exploited Children (NCMEC), reports of online child exploitation surged by 97 percent between 2017 and 2019, and in 2020, there were more than 21.7 million reports of suspected child sexual exploitation, the most ever, further emphasizing the urgent need for action (O'Donnell, 2021). Given the severity of the issue, families and schools must take proactive steps to protect students from deceptive apps and websites.

Schools can help educate students and parents about the potential risks associated with deceptive apps and websites, helping them stay informed about the latest trends and developments. Organizations such as the NCMEC and the Federal Trade Commission offer resources and guidelines to help parents navigate this complex landscape; schools can help raise awareness about these resources and connect families to them.

- Parenting, Media, and Everything in Between (Common Sense Media, n.d.a)
- Parents' Ultimate Guides (Common Sense Media, n.d.b)
- FTC Provides Back-to-School Advice for Parents (Federal Trade Commission, 2018)
- 15 Dangerous Apps Parents Need to Know About, According to Law Enforcement (Mejia, 2022)
- Keeping Students Safe Online (U.S. Department of Education, 2024)
- AI Is Making Data Literacy a "Survival Skill" That Schools Must Teach, Experts Argue (Langreo, 2023)

While many of these are aimed at parents and caregivers, they contain useful information for educators, and principals can share them with the school community, including families, to help ensure that everyone is aware.

Cyberbullying

Studies have highlighted the growing concerns related to social media use among young people. For instance, according to a survey conducted by the Pew Research Center (Anderson & Jiang, 2018), 95 percent of teenagers have access to a smartphone, and 45 percent are online almost constantly. Furthermore, a poll by the University of Michigan (2017) finds that 59 percent of teens have experienced some form of cyberbullying. According to Langreo (2023), there have been several reported instances of students using AI tools to generate fake pornographic images of their classmates and fake videos of their teachers or principals, and it seems to be occurring across different student groups.

Administrators should take all allegations of cyberbullying seriously and investigate the claims. Once a claim of cyberbullying is made, the school should initiate an investigation and ascertain if legal authorities should be called. Make arrangements for the students in question to remain separated pending the investigation. Once all the evidence is gathered, notification of findings should be made to the parties involved. Note that these cases are complex, and often, evidence is fleeting. Share findings and discipline students according to policy. Disciplinary policies can be deterrents, but they cannot undo some of the trauma experienced by victims of online harassment, bullying, and deepfakes. Figure 8.1 shows an example of a cyberbullying policy. An investigation template is provided in figure 8.2 (page 150).

Definition of Cyberbullying

The Nadaburg Unified School District is committed to providing a safe and respectful environment for all students, staff, and stakeholders. Cyberbullying disrupts the educational process and the well-being of individuals within our community. This policy outlines the district's definition of cyberbullying, prohibited behaviors, reporting procedures, and consequences for violations.

Cyberbullying includes, but is not limited to, the use of electronic communication devices such as social media platforms, text messaging, email, gaming platforms, or websites to engage in actions that:

- Harass, intimidate, humiliate, or threaten another individual.
- Disseminate false or harmful information about another individual.
- Deliberately exclude, manipulate, or ostracize someone in a harmful manner.

Cyberbullying may occur during or outside school hours, on or off school premises, if it negatively impacts the school environment or the educational process.

Prohibited Behaviors

The following actions are prohibited under this policy.

1. Sending threatening, vulgar, or harassing messages.
2. Posting or sharing embarrassing, false, or private information about someone without consent.
3. Using another person's identity or account to cause harm.
4. Engaging in online actions that encourage exclusion or social isolation of a student or staff member.
5. Creating or sharing harmful content through memes, images, or videos targeting another individual.

Reporting Procedures

1. For Students
    - Students who experience or witness cyberbullying should report incidents to a teacher, counselor, or school administrator immediately.
    - Reports can also be submitted anonymously through the district's online reporting system or suggestion boxes located on campus.
2. For Staff and Parents/Guardians
    - Staff or parents who are aware of cyberbullying incidents must report them to the school principal or designee.
3. Investigative Procedures
    - Upon receiving a report, school administrators will:
        - Document the incident in writing.
        - Notify all relevant parties, including parents/guardians of the involved students.
        - Investigate the matter promptly and confidentially.
4. The investigation may include reviewing electronic communications, interviewing witnesses, and consulting with district IT personnel.

Consequences for Violations

Consequences for engaging in cyberbullying will align with the district's code of conduct and may include:

1. Verbal or written warnings.
2. Parental notification and meetings.
3. Loss of school privileges, including technology or internet access.

Source: Nadaburg Unified School District, 2024. Used with permission.
Figure 8.1: Sample cyberbullying policy.

continued →

4. Restorative justice practices, such as mediation or counseling.
5. Suspension, expulsion, or alternative education placement for severe or repeated incidents.
6. Referral to law enforcement if the behavior violates state or federal laws.

Prevention and Education

1. The district will provide age-appropriate digital citizenship and cyberbullying prevention education annually to students.
2. Staff will receive professional development on identifying and addressing cyberbullying.
3. Parents/guardians will have access to resources and workshops on supporting students' safe use of technology.

Legal References

This policy complies with state and federal laws, including but not limited to:

- The Children's Internet Protection Act (CIPA)
- The Family Educational Rights and Privacy Act (FERPA)

Principal's Investigation

Investigator Name: _____ Position or Title: _____

Date of Report: _____

1. Basic Information
    - Name of individual or individuals reporting the incident:
    _____

    - Date and time the incident was reported:
    _____

    - Method of reporting (for example, verbal, written, online, or anonymous):
    _____

    - Name of alleged target or targets:
    _____

    - Name of alleged perpetrator or perpetrators:
    _____

2. Summary of the Reported Incident
    - Brief description of the reported cyberbullying behavior (include the type of device or platform used, if known):
    _____
    _____
    _____

    - Date and time the incident or incidents occurred (if known):
    _____

    - Location (if applicable): _____

3. Evidence Collected
   (Attach copies where applicable, such as screenshots, emails, or other digital content.)
   - Screenshots, messages, or posts
   - Witness accounts (attach written statements)
   - Other evidence: _____
   _____
   _____
   _____

4. Parties Interviewed
   - Target or targets:
     - Name or names: _____
     - Date and time of interview: _____
     - Summary of statements: _____
     _____
     _____
     _____
   - Perpetrator or perpetrators:
     - Name or names: _____
     - Date and time of interview: _____
     - Summary of statements: _____
     _____
     _____
     _____
   - Witness or witnesses:
     - Name or names: _____
     - Date and time of interview: _____
     - Summary of statements: _____
     _____
     _____
     _____

5. Investigation Findings
   - Did the behavior meet the definition of cyberbullying under district policy?
     ☐ Yes
     ☐ No
     Explain:
     _____
     _____
     _____

Figure 8.2: Cyberbullying incident investigation template.

continued →

- Were other policy violations identified? (If yes, specify):
  - ☐ Yes
  - ☐ No
  - Explain: _____
  _____
  _____

6. Actions Taken
   - Notifications:
     - ☐ Parents or guardians of target or targets notified (date and time): _____
     - ☐ Parents or guardians of perpetrator or perpetrators notified (date and time): _____
   - Consequences for perpetrator or perpetrators:
     - ☐ Verbal warning
     - ☐ Written warning
     - ☐ Loss of privileges (specify): _____
     - ☐ Counseling or restorative justice (specify): _____
     - ☐ Suspension or expulsion (specify duration): _____
     - ☐ Referral to law enforcement
   - Support for target or targets:
     - ☐ Counseling
     - ☐ Academic adjustments (if applicable)
     - ☐ Other (specify): _____

7. Resolution and Follow-Up
   - Date incident resolved: _____
   - Follow-up dates to ensure resolution and monitor well-being:
   _____
   _____
   _____

Investigator Signature: _____ Date: _____

Source: Nadaburg Unified School District, 2024. Used with permission.

School Social Media Policy

A school social media policy outlines guidelines for students, staff, and administrators on how to appropriately use social media platforms while representing the school, emphasizing responsible online behavior, protecting student privacy, and maintaining a professional image, including restrictions on sharing personal information, bullying, and inappropriate content. Enlisting stakeholders and legal authority to craft your social media policies for students and staff can be time well spent. A guide from an organization such as Common Sense Media (n.d.b) can help parents and educators better understand the attraction and characteristics of social media platforms that are popular with students. A sound social media policy is necessary for both educators in their professional and personal capacities and for use by students. Along with those stakeholders whose input you deem most valuable, I would advise bringing legal authorities into the discussion as well. First, make sure everyone understands the current popular apps and types of apps. Then, review examples.

Popular Social Media Platforms

Trying to create policy around specific apps is a losing battle since new ones become popular very quickly, and others fall by the wayside. Focusing on types of social media platforms can help school policies be more effective. For example, a rule against sharing videos will be more far-reaching than a rule banning TikTok.

- **Social networks:** These allow users to share their thoughts, create groups based on shared interests, and engage in discussions. These often include the ability to upload photos and videos and share links to spark discussion.

- **Discussion forums:** These are text-based platforms that may include channels or individual forums for various topics or interests. Through these avenues, users chat or engage in thread-based discussions. Some may include limited image sharing. Community building is a big part of these forums, but users are often anonymous.

- **Image-sharing networks:** These enable users to share photos and short videos. These can offer endless opportunities for creativity and originality and have gained immense popularity among young people, fostering creativity and providing a sense of community. Some types of content "disappear" after a short period, a widely popular feature due to its temporary and interactive nature. However, users can screenshot and otherwise save content, meaning anything that is shared in such a way should not be assumed to be gone.

- **Video-sharing platforms:** These allow users to interact through comments, direct messages, and live streams. This type is widely popular, providing people with a platform for self-expression and visual storytelling.

Policy Examples

Schools or districts should create clear policies about social media use, including by students and staff members; cover them in preservice; and include them in the handbook. An example of a school's social media policy appears in figure 8.3.

Social Media Policies and Communication Guidelines

This handbook provides guidelines and policies for teachers and staff members of public elementary and high schools regarding the use of social media and communication with students on these platforms. It emphasizes the importance of maintaining professionalism, protecting student privacy, and adhering to legal and ethical standards. The purpose of these policies is to ensure a safe and respectful online environment for all students and educators.

Social Media Usage Policies

1. Personal Social Media Accounts:
   a. Teachers and staff members are encouraged to maintain personal social media accounts responsibly.
   b. It is important to remember that personal posts can reflect on the school and profession; therefore, exercise caution when posting content that could be deemed inappropriate or unprofessional.
   c. Avoid sharing any information that could compromise student privacy or violate confidentiality agreements.
2. School-Related Social Media Accounts:
   a. Teachers and staff members who manage official school-related social media accounts must adhere to the guidelines provided by the school administration.
   b. Ensure that all posts are accurate, respectful, and align with the educational mission and values of the school.
   c. Obtain proper consent for publishing student images, names, or any identifiable information.
3. Social Media Etiquette:
   a. Maintain a professional tone and language when interacting with students, colleagues, and parents on social media platforms.
   b. Refrain from engaging in online arguments or sharing controversial opinions that could negatively impact your professional standing.
   c. Be mindful of the potential consequences of sharing information or images that could be misinterpreted or misconstrued.

Communication With Students on Social Media

1. Teacher-Student Interaction:
   a. Teachers should primarily use official school communication channels (for example, email, online platforms) for academic-related conversations with students.
   b. Limited interactions on social media platforms can be acceptable for educational purposes, such as sharing relevant resources or facilitating class discussions.
   c. Teachers must maintain appropriate boundaries and avoid engaging in personal or confidential discussions with students on social media.

2. Connecting With Students on Social Media:
   a. Teachers and staff members should refrain from connecting with current students on personal social media accounts.
   b. In exceptional cases where a social media connection is necessary (for example, extracurricular activities), obtain written consent from the student's parent or guardian.
   c. Remember that engaging with students on social media can blur professional boundaries and potentially expose both parties to risks.

Perils of Posting or Following Minors on Social Media

Research has revealed several perils associated with posting or following minors on social media. These risks include:

1. Privacy Invasion—According to a research review by Adwait S Malik, Sourya Acharya, and Sonal Humane (2024), posting or sharing images of minors without their consent can result in privacy invasion and potential harm to their psychological well-being.
2. Cyberbullying—A research article by Justin W. Patchin and Sameer Hinduja (2021) highlights the increased vulnerability of minors to cyberbullying when interacting with adults on social media. This can have severe emotional and psychological consequences for the students involved.
3. Grooming and Predatory Behavior—Numerous studies, such as the one conducted by Janis Wolak, David Finkelhor, and Kimberly J. Mitchell (2012), have demonstrated the potential for adults to engage in predatory behavior and exploitation when they have access to minors through social media platforms.

By adhering to the policies outlined in this handbook, teachers and staff members play a crucial role in ensuring a safe and respectful online environment for students. Understanding the potential risks associated with social media usage and communication with minors is essential for maintaining a professional and responsible online presence. Let us work together to create a positive digital learning community that promotes student well-being and academic success.

[School Principal signature]

Source: Adapted from Arizona State Board of Education, 2022.
Figure 8.3: Sample social media policy.

Considering the fast-changing world of technology and social media, I would suggest involving both information technology teams and local law enforcement in regular conversations about social media dangers. The main objective of the school's social media policy should always be the safety of school employees and students. Beyond the specific school policy, principals should make sure that staff members are aware of expectations for their own use of social media, both personal and related to their work in the school. Some schools embrace the use of social media as a tool for engaging with students and connecting with families and the greater community, but rules must be in place to ensure that everyone is safe. See figure 8.4 (page 156) for an example.

School Policies
- Make sure you know social media guidelines for your school or district.
- Share and discuss your social media guidelines with students.
- Provide consent and opt-out forms for parents and caregivers.
- Be aware of students whose parents or caregivers haven't given consent.

Devices and Accounts
- Keep personal and professional accounts separate.
- Check and adjust privacy and security settings on your social media accounts.
- Find out which social media platforms your students use and learn what you can about them, even if you don't use them.
- Look at your bio and profile information and revise as needed to ensure privacy.
- When coming up with account names or handles, avoid using first or last names.
- Look into photo-editing tools so that you're able to edit out, blur, or obscure sensitive information.
- Audit your settings for sharing your content regularly.
- Check your photo settings and be sure the option for location data is turned off.
- Social media content can be archived or deleted, and you can do so at intervals to protect your privacy.
- Don't provide personal information to anyone over social media, even people you know.
- Before posting, check wording and attachments for sensitive items, including names, contact information, academic records, location information, student faces, handwriting, and school or district names.

Families
- Make families aware of your policies, especially when they post on school social media.
- Consider hosting an event for families to encourage the responsible use of social media at school and at home.

Classroom Spaces
- Consider using a classroom-only technology, such as a learning management system or messaging app, to share information safely and practice digital citizenship.

Source: © 2024 by Desere Hockman and Aspasia Angelou. Used with permission. Adapted from Higgin, 2022.
Figure 8.4: Example of social media school rules.

Conclusion

There is no doubt that social media has introduced ways for technology to enhance our connections despite geographical separation and time zones, forging connections that were formerly logistically impossible. The power of social media and technology has also broken down barriers of culture and economics—virtually everyone you meet has a communication device. This avenue into other people's worlds has also made us more vulnerable to data breaches, scams, impersonation, and harassment than ever before. The role of a school principal in navigating these innovations is fraught with risks—both legal and ethical. Be informed, be reflective, and be collaborative in discussing the pros and cons of creating policies and structures to support ways that technology and social media can enhance learning and reduce harm.

Chapter 9

Reflection

As a principal, you may feel simultaneously like a hummingbird in constant motion and as though you were standing still and accomplishing little by the end of the day. Without reflection, you can feel unbalanced and allow small, important details to fall through the cracks. To remedy this, I make an annual gift to my employees and leadership of a small journal to help them understand that the habit of jotting down notes throughout the day will bring immeasurable peace of mind. I use my own journal for a fifteen-minute reflection time at the end of the day, to follow up with parents and staff via email or phone, and to guide my own thinking for upcoming conversations and next steps. I also use it to jot down first moves for the next day, training opportunities, and long-term ideas.

Speaking from a legal standpoint, the notes a principal takes in a parent, student, or staff meeting can be subpoenaed for years to come. I had a lawsuit that requested any and all notes on a student bullying case three years after the student was enrolled. Going back and reviewing those notes was invaluable and helped guide the district's defense team. Do not try to start your daily notes on a new tablet or sticky note every day without ensuring that you are adding those to your annual journal or making an electronic notation if you choose to have the electronic format—inevitably, a note will be lost or forgotten. It's a habit that will pay dividends. Once a journal is full, I make sure to note the date and time it is put on the shelf, in a box, or in a drawer. Then, I start a new journal.

When it comes to reflection, there are two important facets: (1) looking deeply within and finding strength in isolation—what might feel like the unique loneliness of your position—and (2) looking without to build a strong, steady network of fellow leaders, mentors, and thought partners. Both are necessary for success as a priority school principal.

The Loneliness of the Priority School Principal

Criticism can often be difficult to unpack and digest, but reflection in isolation can help one to step back and recognize room for improvement in a safe way. In the realm of education, continuous improvement is vital for the success of both students and educators. To foster a culture of growth and learning at every level, school leaders need to establish a habit of professional reflection. They need a structured framework for self-assessment, goal setting, and ongoing development. Professional reflection serves as a valuable mechanism for educators to reflect on their daily practice, identify areas of strength, and pinpoint areas for growth. By engaging in regular self-reflection, leaders can enhance their instructional strategies, improve student outcomes, and foster a collaborative learning environment. Research indicates that educators increasingly feel like their "brain feels like a browser with 100 tabs open" (Kim, Oxley, & Asbury, 2022).

As mentioned, each year, I give my leadership team a journal to use for thoughts, ideas, and next steps to make note of throughout the day. I ask them to use this as a teacher would use an exit ticket in the classroom: What questions remain after the workday? What do you want to remember to do first thing the next morning? Who do you need to call or email as a follow-through? I also ask them to reflect on additional questions: How did you build relationships? How did you damage relationships? I have found that they are often ready for another gift by the winter break because the first journal is full! An added benefit is the peace of mind that comes with making notes that then allow you to let your mind rest in the evening or over the weekend.

Some topics I suggest for reflection logs include the following.

- **Key takeaways from leadership meetings:** What do I need to share with staff from a leadership or district-level meeting?

- **Questions to follow up on with staff or parents:** Who do I need to follow up with regarding a student situation, and which teachers or staff do I need input from?

- **Training and support needed based on observations:** What did I see in classrooms? Is there additional professional development that I can offer?

- **Collaborative conversations I need to schedule:** Which teams need to convene based on the calendar of events?

- **Supportive feedback and coaching conversations I need to set up:** Regular check-ins and one-on-one meetings can contribute to the growth and development of employees, fostering a culture of continuous improvement. I prefer to have quick face-to-face check-ins with every employee in the organization to build a relationship of mutual trust.

Creating a habit of reviewing the reflection log at the end of the day and making notes for priority items to follow up on first thing in the morning is an essential habit of getting organized. A lack of follow-through is a complaint I have heard from teachers, staff, and parents alike. With all the browsers open, it's hardly possible to revisit mental notes from each situation. Writing down those notes and next steps is a game-changer for a priority school leader.

The principal's time log from chapter 5 (see figure 5.1, page 102) is also useful for personal reflection on how much time you are spending observing instruction, handling discipline, working on emails, visiting collaborative teams, and facilitating teacher and staff discussions. Reflecting on and organizing your time will also help you be more efficient with the time needed while students and staff are present.

Part of looking within is examining how you are balancing your work and your personal life, as well as reflecting deeply on your purpose and the meaning of credibility.

Work-Life Balance

The balance between work and home life is critical for the marathon life of a priority school principal. Brigid Schulte (2018), an author and expert on work-life balance, writes:

> What we see—our role models—shape what we think is possible. And right now, so many of us are stuck in the workplace overworking because that's all we see in our leaders. So perhaps, if we are to change, what we need are fewer breathless articles about inhuman and insane CEO schedules that ignore the costs to health, families, and, ultimately, innovation and business productivity.

The parallels to priority schools are many. There will rarely, if ever, be a day where a priority school principal feels that they did everything well. You will need a network of support and an intentional stress outlet. I know from personal experience that if you do not make time for yourself, your health, and your family, the burden of the physical, mental, and emotional toll of the job will force you to do so. Be proactive.

One of the best lessons I learned over time and experience as a priority school principal is that the work will continue each day. Prioritize safety and be able to observe instruction to take the necessary steps for academic improvement. Ensure you have face time with teachers and the guiding coalition to keep relationships at the forefront of your work.

Understanding that you cannot endure the sprints within your day, as well as the marathon of the weeks and year, means truly modeling balance. Save drafts of emails to avoid losing your thoughts, but don't send work directives and information over the weekend. Remember that positional authority is always at play, and whether you intend to create urgency in the moment or not, an email from the principal on Sunday morning can wreak havoc on personal time or family time.

Purpose and Credibility

As a principal, one often has to go back to personal core values and beliefs in dealing with staff and teachers. Why? Because in the face of dishonesty or a lack of gratitude, leaders can get to a place of feeling depleted, continually pouring into others without having the same reciprocated from those they serve. This is where our purpose and self-trust come into play. It's interesting to see that to increase credibility and influence, we must know ourselves first and always behave in such a way as to reinforce our own integrity. In doing so, our credibility and trustworthiness will inevitably be undeniable. As leaders, we live under a microscope where the alignment of words and actions are the litmus test of our trustworthiness.

In the afterword of *The Speed of Trust*, Stephen R. Covey (2018) writes:

> **Trust is the new currency in today's connected, collaborative world. Contrary to what most people think, creating trust is a learnable skill. When trust is low, individuals become suspicious of each other, their boss, and of the organization. They guard communication, speculate and disengage. As a result, productivity grinds to a crawl and costs increase. (p. 342)**

Practicing communication transparently, directly, and respectfully is how we build a sense of understanding and credibility. As leaders, it is true that we often view trust as an intangible and ambiguous emotion rather than a measurable skill. Changing our mindset is a critical first step in altering how we approach our relationships as leaders and on a personal level. In education, we have the responsibility of recognizing that trust in our adult interactions will inevitably affect our students. I asked multiple colleagues, family, and friends about the notion of loyalty. The responses are very intriguing. To summarize the discussion, as an organization, especially an educational entity entrusted *in loco parentis*, we must be loyal to our core values and mission rather than to a person. However, human organizations often work on a sort of fake loyalty that looks more like obedience because trust is absent. Credibility comes from character and competence, and from credibility and respect comes trust. True loyalty requires both respect and belief that a leader will operate from a place of integrity regardless of personal gain or loss.

Merriam-Webster's online dictionary defines *loyalty* (n.d.) as "fidelity, allegiance, fealty, devotion, or piety which binds one to duty in the face of any temptation to renounce, desert, or betray." So, how do school leaders address unethical behavior in the face of this definition? This enduring question has led me to the conclusion that we must be loyal to our highest belief or purpose and not to people or organizations. To be clear, this doesn't mean one should bypass the channels of investigative conversation and allow for the rectification of wrongs, but it does mean we confront hard topics and seek to bring all evidence to the table. Thereby, we can be loyal to our purpose and not fall into a Machiavellian, ends-justify-the-means mental rabbit hole.

Reflection With Mentors and Thought Partners

If the district does not provide adequate leadership coaching and mentoring opportunities, a principal can seek a professional who can be a thought partner or mentor. The job is isolating even under the best circumstances—in priority schools, this is even more true. Leadership development specialist Janet T. Phan (2021) writes that a trusted mentor can be instrumental in helping you see the path forward and options for decision making when you lack confidence or experience. When I was a new principal in a priority school, Sharon Kramer mentored me by talking through problems of practice, helped me prepare for difficult conversations, and guided me on to the next steps for professional development.

Cultivating a professional learning network through organizations can be extremely helpful in alleviating the isolation that comes with school leadership, but there may not be many experienced and successful priority school principals among those you meet at conferences. With experience comes seniority, and that often means that leaders choose to move out of the most high-needs and difficult schools. Simply put, principals burn out due to the endless hours, weak support, and demands that weigh heavily on them emotionally, spiritually, and physically.

Looking within or outside your district at higher-level directors or central administration personnel who have been in your shoes can help you identify a mentor. Be proactive and make time for a relationship that is not supervisory. Sometimes, social networks and groups on social media can help you find a professional support network. Don't be discouraged if it takes more than one try to find the right group. Be prepared to take what advice and ideas you need and let the naysayers go. Inevitably, you will find people who cannot be solution-minded in any group online or in person.

Consultants, such as the school and content-area coaches with Solution Tree, can also be helpful in talking through your ideas and concerns if they are directly related to the mutual work: School culture, leadership development, professional learning communities, and academic interventions are just some of the topics that can help you foster a thought partnership or mentorship. Don't be afraid to ask for supportive conversations. Most practitioners understand the challenges as they have also lived the life of a school leader. We know that isolation is real, and you must actively work to stay connected as a priority school leader.

Conclusion

I think it is quite appropriate that the final chapter of this book comes down to trust—it serves both as the foundation and the roof that shelters us in the unbelievably difficult job of being a priority school principal. Every day, we are tested and watched to see if we are going to build trust by following through on our promises, and every night, we consider how we eroded or increased trust in our teams. It is the hardest but also the most rewarding of jobs. I know that I will never look back on being a priority school principal without gratitude and a bit of romanticizing the struggle; we are in the business of making the most important investment of all: people.

Epilogue

Purpose Will Bring You Full Circle

This book was written for the practitioners—the boots on the ground. After my role as a priority school principal, I was exhausted but simultaneously fulfilled. I remember calling two of my closest principal friends after my move to Tulsa as a district-level administrator because we needed to talk about what felt so surreal: how we had worked tirelessly and what we had learned about our leadership roles but never really had time or a safe environment to process. One friend, Ashley, was retiring from the principalship. I was moving to be a district director, but we both wanted our experiences to help other principals, both in priority schools and diverse settings, and we knew they could. We agreed that, in hindsight, we felt isolated and unsure of our decisions. We hoped that we were making the best decisions in many instances and wished for something, a guide of sorts, that would be a one-stop shop for resources. After three years of making notes for this book, I finally decided I was ready to write a practical handbook with usable templates that address the types of issues that my colleagues and I have faced.

I thought about all the tools I had created out of necessity and all those that I still share today as a certified associate for Solution Tree. As a superintendent, many of these templates and tools have gone through iterations to improve on specificity and need. We are in the human business, and humans can always surprise you with new problems—and new solutions! My final thought on this book is the hope that it can alleviate some questions, bring reassurance, and be a critical thought partner for the lonely but most important leadership position: the priority school principal. You are the captain of your ship. You help set the course every day for student learning, an inclusive environment, and a culture where no students will fall through the cracks created by averages or outdated policies. This work is hard, and it may seem endless, yet it is also the most gratifying position you can have to influence the lasting outcomes in the lives of young people. You will be forever changed, my friend.

Appendix

Personalized Principal's Calendar

The personalized calendar that follows on page 170 is intended to help you plan ahead and be intentional with assigning tasks or preparing for events. There are additional options to add more items that pertain to your site's specific culture: traditions and opportunities to build a collaborative community with business partners, parents, teachers, and students. When communication is timely, teachers don't have to feel reactionary to last-minute requests or preparations. You can help them be reflective and intentional by creating a supportive school culture. The calendar also helps the guiding coalition plan for communication to go out to families and students who may have children at multiple schools and need to plan for engagement and participation. For priority school principals, organization is key to timely and effective communications.

This calendar can be tailored to include more subheadings if those apply to your context, but I tried to include the activities that are all part of leadership in schools: planning, preparing, meeting, and communicating. In the role of principal, every day is different, so if you can plan for the events of the month, you can move out of the constant feeling of putting out fires but be prepared when you need to because the routine events are systematic.

Personalized Principal's Calendar

JULY

IDENTIFY, REVIEW, AND UPDATE

- ☐ Update and add course sections to the master schedule based on projected enrollment and student course selections.
- ☐ Review staffing via budgeted full and part-time positions (certified and support).
- ☐ Review horizontal collaboration times and teacher planning times.
- ☐ Review scope and sequence and district curriculums maps.
- ☐ Set times for the guiding coalition to meet.
- ☐ Review times for Tier 3 intervention during the school day, plan for the data to be used for grouping, and add to the schedule rotation.
- ☐ Review the walkthrough checklist (figure 5.2, page 103) and ensure administrators have training credentials.
- ☐ Update and replace classroom emergency flip charts and maps as needed.

PREPARE, PLAN, AND COMMUNICATE

- ☐ Review spring assessment data and related professional development.
- ☐ Map out a review of the school's mission and vision related to school and district goals.
- ☐ Plan for the first week of school and draft related communications for teachers, staff, and families.
- ☐ Finalize class lists and communicate with special education teacher leaders to send IEPs to necessary personnel (teachers and aides).
- ☐ Organize and set meetings with all building-level committees; communicate dates and times via a shared calendar.
- ☐ Meet with parent-teacher organizations and booster clubs to plan for annual events (meet the teacher, student and teacher awards, celebrations, student showcases, and extracurricular events).
- ☐ Review last-minute vacancies, if needed.
- ☐ Set observation schedule for the year during appropriate windows.
- ☐ Communicate via the school website and social media: supply lists, handbooks, back-to-school letters, and annual student at-a-glance calendars.
- ☐ _____
- ☐ _____
- ☐ _____

AUGUST

IDENTIFY, REVIEW, AND UPDATE

- ☐ Review state testing achievement data and plan for sharing with teachers and staff.
- ☐ Using data, set personal and professional goals and the guiding coalition goals.
- ☐ Plan to review and practice safety plan with the staff.
- ☐ Ensure all safety measures and communications are in working order; communicate with district facilities and operations team.
- ☐ Plan all emergency drills for the year and add them to the calendar with guiding coalition invites.
- ☐ Review annual budget and expenditure needs with appropriate site and district personnel.
- ☐ Review and communicate first-day procedures and share with leadership, transportation, nutrition services, and office staff.
- ☐ Review purchase orders and identify missing materials; notify business office personnel.
- ☐ Notify staff of any master schedule or teacher assignment changes.
- ☐ Ensure that staff and student handbooks are printed or shared electronically for distribution. Verify that families have indicated receipt with a signature.
- ☐ Ensure families or students sign an acceptable use policy for technology devices and insurance.
- ☐ Identify new teacher mentors and pair with new teachers.
- ☐ _____
- ☐ _____
- ☐ _____

PLAN, PREPARE, AND COMMUNICATE

- ☐ Plan and review fall benchmark testing and communicate with the assessment committee or site coordinator.
- ☐ Set testing staff meeting on a shared calendar.
- ☐ Plan and set weekly meetings with the guiding coalition, principal's administrative assistant, assistant principal, teacher leaders, learning acceleration specialist, counselor, or other site-level personnel. Communicate with a shared calendar.
- ☐ Create or update weekly communication templates, meeting agenda templates, and leadership meeting norms and commitments.
- ☐ Schedule time to meet with new teachers and other staff new to the building.

- ☐ Organize your office, desk, and plan book or note keeper.
- ☐ Review or draft your theme and inspirational remarks for the teachers and staff.
- ☐ Update and review the opening intercom announcements to include a theme and key messages to set the tone for the day.
- ☐ Communicate with staff for the first week's enrollment counts and forms to be collected or turned in to the office.
- ☐ Leave a preprinted welcome note or token in each teacher and staff mailbox for the first day.
- ☐ Create and communicate the duty schedule.
- ☐ Add leadership and personal duty times to the calendar, including morning cafeteria and bus duty, passing periods, lunch and recess times, after-school bus duty, and after-school extracurricular activities or athletics.
- ☐ Greet new families and students who come to obtain a schedule or learn about the school.
- ☐ Have counselors assign a buddy student to new students.
- ☐ Plan to visit all classrooms on the first day of school.
- ☐ Develop or update general building forms as needed.
- ☐ Post all major events, athletics, after-school schedules for tutoring, and holidays on the school's website calendar.
- ☐ Delegate webmaster, social media lead, other key staff, and leadership duties as needed; assign rights to those delegated.
- ☐ Review positive behavior interventions and support procedures and meeting dates, share with the committee, and plan for full staff communication.
- ☐ Clarify discipline procedures and what constitutes an office referral.
- ☐ Assign and update campus bulletin boards; ensure all outdated materials and flyers are removed.
- ☐ Review the first monthly governing board report from the principal's site preparation and school opening.
- ☐ Review collaborative team meeting norms and agendas; send updates.
- ☐ _____
- ☐ _____
- ☐ _____

SCHEDULE AND MEET

- ☐ Meet with building custodians to clarify expectations.
- ☐ Notify the fire department and central office of your drill schedule; plan for debriefs.

- [ ] Schedule student grade-level meetings to clarify rules and expectations.
- [ ] Send curriculum maps and state standards to new teachers.
- [ ] _____
- [ ] _____
- [ ] _____

SEPTEMBER

IDENTIFY, REVIEW, AND UPDATE

- [ ] Review assessment schedules and check on pacing with curriculum maps and lesson plans in walkthroughs.
- [ ] Identify struggling teachers and monitor progress.
- [ ] Identify struggling students and monitor progress for possible MTSS action.
- [ ] Modify the observation schedule for the year as needed.
- [ ] Identify instructional strategies that are succeeding and ask teachers to share them during staff meetings for professional development.
- [ ] Identify morning and afternoon drop-off and pick-up bottlenecks to adjust for traffic flow.
- [ ] _____
- [ ] _____
- [ ] _____

PREPARE AND PLAN

- [ ] Communicate the fall events calendar to staff and families.
- [ ] Issue safety committee invitation and agenda based on shared emergency response plan.
- [ ] Based on observations, plan for hard conversations with faculty or staff not aligned with the school's vision and goals.
- [ ] Review the monthly governing board report.
- [ ] _____
- [ ] _____
- [ ] _____

The Principal's Handbook for Priority Schools in a PLC at Work® © 2025 Solution Tree Press • SolutionTree.com
Visit **go.SolutionTree.com/priorityschools** to download this free reproducible.

DEVELOP AND COMMUNICATE

- ☐ Create teams or committees to tackle schoolwide events, such as community and board showcase evenings.
- ☐ Review positive behavior interventions and support data teams to tackle issues indicated by discipline referrals (time, frequency, grade level, and location indicating patterns) for possible duty station or intervention.
- ☐ Prepare for fall benchmarks and staff meetings regarding procedures.
- ☐ Communicate with families of students not on track.
- ☐ _____
- ☐ _____
- ☐ _____

MEET AND CONDUCT

- ☐ Meet with parent-teacher organization or parent-teacher-student association to plan for recognition and awards for fall sports and academics.
- ☐ Meet with teachers to set professional educator goal plans for the year.
- ☐ Meet with new teachers and staff whose employment started after the first day to ensure onboarding has been seamless.
- ☐ Conduct first emergency drills and debrief with school and district staff.
- ☐ Meet with students by grade level to reinforce expectations.
- ☐ Meet with teachers to review educator goal plans or student learning objectives.
- ☐ Meet with substitute teachers to discuss expectations.
- ☐ _____
- ☐ _____
- ☐ _____

OCTOBER

IDENTIFY, REVIEW, AND UPDATE

- ☐ Update monitoring on struggling students and assign to interventions or MTSS review.
- ☐ Ensure that by October 1, the student count for the state department of education is accurate.
- ☐ Review collaborative team meeting artifacts with guiding coalition.
- ☐ Discuss classroom walkthrough impressions and wonderings with the guiding coalition.

- [ ] Confirm new teachers have been onboarded into collaborative team cycles and understand purpose and process.
- [ ] _____
- [ ] _____
- [ ] _____

DEFINE AND COMMUNICATE

- [ ] Reiterate lesson plan expectations and submittal to administration.
- [ ] Communicate with families and students about upcoming events and assessments.
- [ ] Communicate with club and organization sponsors to ensure financial obligations are being processed according to policy; answer questions for new sponsors.
- [ ] Check in with new teachers, staff, and mentors.
- [ ] Review the monthly governing board report.
- [ ] Communicate winter athletics, tryouts, and extracurriculars to students and families via website and social media.
- [ ] _____
- [ ] _____
- [ ] _____

SCHEDULE AND MEET

- [ ] Meet with department and collaborative team leaders, teacher leaders, and learning acceleration specialists to look at data and plan for goals and targeted interventions for individuals and small groups.
- [ ] Conduct emergency drills.
- [ ] Meet with athletic directors to make sure that facilities are reserved and ready for events. Attend on nights when multiple events happen simultaneously for maximum exposure. Remember to take pictures for your social media networks, website, and hallway bulletin boards.
- [ ] Reflect on your performance for the first quarter. What has gone well? Where can you improve?
- [ ] _____
- [ ] _____
- [ ] _____

NOVEMBER

IDENTIFY, REVIEW, AND UPDATE

- ☐ Review your district's policies regarding holiday activities and displays. Update staff on food allergens before purchases are made for holiday celebrations.
- ☐ Monitor your own progress. Make sure you're moving forward in areas where you will be evaluated.
- ☐ Set your own observations based on evaluated domains with your evaluator.
- ☐ Review site office and classroom phone lists and extensions to ensure they are updated. Send to staff if there are changes.
- ☐ Appraise staff development provided to date and revise; expand plans as analysis indicates.
- ☐ Review monthly governing board report and special first-quarter highlights.
- ☐ _____
- ☐ _____
- ☐ _____

MEET AND HOLD

- ☐ Conduct school emergency drills as required.
- ☐ Meet with teams for updates on student progress for interventions.
- ☐ Prepare and share winter event schedules and coverages as needed.
- ☐ Hold (quarterly as appropriate to building) data team meetings to review benchmark results, grade reports, student work, and other data. Discuss progress toward goals with the entire staff.
- ☐ _____
- ☐ _____
- ☐ _____

DECEMBER

IDENTIFY, REVIEW, AND UPDATE

- ☐ Review your district's policy for teacher evaluations and growth plans or collective bargaining agreement. Follow prescribed procedures with any teachers whose rating is likely to be ineffective. Consult human resources for clarification and assistance.
- ☐ Identify maintenance issues and tasks for winter break.
- ☐ Review inclement weather schedule procedures and communicate with staff.

- [ ] Identify struggling students and monitor progress.
- [ ] _____
- [ ] _____
- [ ] _____

PREPARE AND PLAN

- [ ] Plan midyear student recognition program. Review qualifications and involve staff in selecting recipients. Calculate the length of the program and develop and announce the assembly schedule in advance.
- [ ] Plan and prepare for second-semester instructional strategies and triage to prepare for spring testing.
- [ ] Prepare second-semester benchmark and exam schedule; communicate to staff.
- [ ] Review the monthly governing board report.
- [ ] _____
- [ ] _____
- [ ] _____

COMMUNICATE

- [ ] Communicate with families by letter if their child has exceeded the district limit on the number of acceptable absences. Inform them about medical excuse requirements and potential academic failure and set up meeting times in person, if needed.
- [ ] Communicate with families by letter if their child is not on track to achieve needed credits for the year.
- [ ] Discuss course offerings to be added to student choice surveys with a counselor.
- [ ] Communicate information on upcoming events to parents by email or mail. Include frequent reminders to update changes in their contact information in case of emergency.
- [ ] For secondary schools, communicate final exam expectations to your staff regarding students who request to take exams early, exam review and preparation, exam dates and times, and so on.
- [ ] _____
- [ ] _____
- [ ] _____

MEET AND HOLD

- [ ] Hold faculty and staff holiday party or recognition event.
- [ ] Conduct midyear staff data analysis.
- [ ] Continue administrative rotation of meetings with all collaborative teams.
- [ ] Send staff survey for first-semester organizational strengths and areas for growth.
- [ ] Meet with the parent-teacher organization or parent-teacher-student association for second-semester planning of events and teacher appreciation week.
- [ ] Conduct school safety drills.
- [ ] Meet with positive behavior interventions and support and social-emotional learning team for review of discipline referrals and next steps.
- [ ] _____
- [ ] _____
- [ ] _____

JANUARY

IDENTIFY, REVIEW, AND UPDATE

- [ ] Review your professional goals for the year and assess the next steps.
- [ ] Review the school goals with the guiding coalition and assess the next steps.
- [ ] Meet with departments to review goals and facilitate discussion for the next steps.
- [ ] Update classroom walkthrough schedule.
- [ ] Update the second-semester calendar on the website and communicate on social media or family email.
- [ ] Schedule the next round of teacher observations during preconferences and postconferences for feedback.
- [ ] Update and close out improvement plans or take them to the next appropriate level for nonrenewal as guided by human resources, collective bargaining agreement, or evaluation policy.
- [ ] Schedule observations with your supervisor.
- [ ] Review the monthly governing board report.
- [ ] Communicate spring activities, athletics, and extracurricular schedules on the website.
- [ ] _____
- [ ] _____
- [ ] _____

MEET AND HOLD

- [ ] Hold (quarterly as appropriate to building) full staff data team meeting to review benchmark results, grade reports, student work, and other data. Discuss progress toward goals.
- [ ] Review first-semester lists of students receiving Ds and Fs and meet with teachers over 15 percent to discuss obstacles to student success.
- [ ] Ensure students who are not making progress have met with counselors and are in small-group intervention groups; monitor progress.
- [ ] Conduct emergency drills.
- [ ] Meet with teachers to review progress on educator goal plans or SLOs.
- [ ] Meet with the site safety team to update plans if needed.
- [ ] Hold spring sponsors' and coaches' meetings.
- [ ] _____
- [ ] _____
- [ ] _____

FEBRUARY

IDENTIFY, REVIEW, AND UPDATE

- [ ] For secondary schools, review high school pretesting procedures for ACT; test practice site for technology.
- [ ] Review spring break guidelines and issue reminders for practices with students.
- [ ] Identify struggling students and monitor progress.
- [ ] Review the plan for the site testing team to prepare classrooms and staff procedures.
- [ ] Update duty stations for spring, as needed.
- [ ] _____
- [ ] _____
- [ ] _____

COMMUNICATE AND MEET

- [ ] Have discussions with borderline teachers (nonrenewal or growth progress discussions).
- [ ] Email or otherwise communicate with the business department regarding spending and budgetary needs for summer school.

- [ ] Email or otherwise communicate with human resources regarding summer and fall staffing.
- [ ] Have discussions with teachers about the plan, timeframe, and resources available to be prepared for roster verification.
- [ ] Meet with the MTSS team to review student progress and next steps.
- [ ] Meet with families regarding students not on track for graduation or promotion; ensure all documentation of letters and conversations is in order.
- [ ] Review the monthly governing board report.
- [ ] _____
- [ ] _____
- [ ] _____

MARCH

DEVELOP, IDENTIFY, REVIEW, AND UPDATE

- [ ] Review spring break guidelines; issue reminders for practices with students.
- [ ] Identify struggling students and monitor progress.
- [ ] Review the plan for the site testing team to prepare classrooms and staff procedures.
- [ ] Update duty stations for spring, as needed.
- [ ] Ensure students who are not making progress have met with counselors and are in small-group intervention groups; monitor progress.
- [ ] _____
- [ ] _____
- [ ] _____

PREPARE AND PLAN

- [ ] Review data for staffing moves.
- [ ] Continue observations and feedback loops.
- [ ] Monitor and adjust plans for improvement.
- [ ] Plan for job fairs.
- [ ] _____
- [ ] _____
- [ ] _____

APRIL

DEVELOP, IDENTIFY, REVIEW, AND UPDATE

- ☐ Start budget planning for the upcoming school year.
- ☐ Build the vision for your summer school program and make sure summer school dates and applications are available to students and families in print and on your website.
- ☐ Counselors should directly contact students who are behind on academic progress or high school credits to ensure they are registering for summer school courses required for graduation.
- ☐ Develop criteria to guide panel selection of new staff members. If you are new to the hiring process, make sure you follow district procedures and human resources hiring guidelines.
- ☐ For secondary schools, develop year-end exam schedules and communicate with staff, families, and students.
- ☐ Identify probable staff vacancies for the next school year via intent-to-return forms.
- ☐ Review needed changes for master scheduling.
- ☐ _____
- ☐ _____
- ☐ _____

PREPARE AND PLAN

- ☐ Submit changes to the student handbook or code of conduct to the superintendent for board of education consideration.
- ☐ Prepare for end-of-year student recognition programs: awards, athletic and extracurricular banquets, presenters, program, and schedule. Collaborate with everyone involved, sponsors, or committees in the planning and facilitation of the events.
- ☐ Review plans for commencement activities.
- ☐ Prepare orders for software purchases at site level and general classroom and office supplies.
- ☐ Review and communicate with grants or purchasing to reserve funds for quality instructional resources to update subscriptions or review with curriculum teams.
- ☐ Plan and prepare for hiring fairs with human resources.
- ☐ _____
- ☐ _____
- ☐ _____

COMMUNICATE AND MEET

☐ Communicate with university partners for student-teacher placements.

☐ Communicate with teachers and staff regarding spring assessment procedures and sign off for understanding.

☐ Schedule the testing final review meeting with the site coordinator.

☐ Communicate with teachers and staff for summative observation meetings and complete scoring rubrics.

☐ Prepare for end-of-year events, determine the coverage needed, and communicate with staff, families, and students.

☐ Ensure promotion and graduation materials are printed and include board members, central office attendees, and speakers.

☐ Meet with parent-teacher organization or parent-teacher-student association to finalize the schedule for end-of-year events, student awards, and teacher and staff appreciation.

☐ Conduct emergency drills and communicate the results of the debrief for any needed revisions to site safety plans.

☐ Hold grade-level meetings to kick off spring assessments.

☐ _____

☐ _____

☐ _____

MAY

DEVELOP, IDENTIFY, REVIEW, AND UPDATE

☐ Identify struggling students and monitor progress (and MTSS if applicable).

☐ Confirm and update all stakeholders on summer school planning, staffing, materials, and transportation.

☐ Confirm final promotion and graduation details.

☐ Complete roster verification and approval.

☐ Finalize summer cleaning, moving, and maintenance needs; update central office facilities and maintenance.

☐ Submit the final record of site emergency drills.

☐ Review and close out improvement plans.

☐ _____

☐ _____

☐ _____

COMMUNICATE AND MEET

- ☐ Send final written determinations of nonpromotion or nongraduation details based on credit completion for state requirements.
- ☐ Discuss with the custodial staff any end-of-year set-up for events, campus clean-up necessary after student dismissal, and summer cleaning schedules.
- ☐ Meet with the athletic director regarding summer camp and summer maintenance scheduling.
- ☐ Communicate and celebrate teacher and staff appreciation week via the website, social media, and email.
- ☐ Meet with the site council for the current year's reflection and next year's planning.
- ☐ Meet with the guiding coalition for reflection activities (stop, continue, and consider).
- ☐ Schedule student locker clean-out; plan device and uniform turn-in times (if applicable) with teacher supervision; communicate with families, staff, and custodians.
- ☐ Update inventories of all site materials and devices.
- ☐ Hold quarterly data meetings with collaborative teams and all staff for summer and fall placements.
- ☐ Send updated enrollment packets to the central office for summer pick-up if school is closed for any period during summer break.
- ☐ _____
- ☐ _____
- ☐ _____

JUNE

DEVELOP, IDENTIFY, REVIEW, AND UPDATE

- ☐ Identify professional goals for the upcoming year.
- ☐ Plan summer rejuvenation time and schedule vacation.
- ☐ Identify professional development priorities for new teachers and staff; plan fall kickoff.
- ☐ Review school and teacher websites (if applicable) for summer learning, reading, or assignments.
- ☐ Ensure all summer athletic camps and tryouts are posted on the website and social media with the coaches' contact information; communicate with facilities and the central office.
- ☐ Make plans for summer receipt of deliveries.

- ☐ Update website, social media, and office exterior with summer office hours, emergency contact information, and enrollment or registration access.
- ☐ Review and start to update the upcoming year's events calendar.
- ☐ Review and update the school improvement plan using the guiding coalition's data analysis and next steps.
- ☐ _____
- ☐ _____
- ☐ _____

COMMUNICATE AND MEET

- ☐ Post positive end-of-year messages to staff, students, and the school community with reminders for summer school and camps.
- ☐ Post pictures and highlights from end-of-year celebrations and events; recognize contributions and valuable partners.
- ☐ Notify staff of dates and times when parts of the building may be inaccessible due to floor waxing, painting, and so on.
- ☐ Change the phone message to include summer office hours and summer school contact information.
- ☐ Monitor and verify postings for vacancies throughout the summer; make sure staff are secured to participate on interview teams.
- ☐ Complete hiring to date and communicate with human resources on loose ends and documents needed.
- ☐ _____
- ☐ _____
- ☐ _____

References and Resources

American School Counselor Association. (2019). *The essential role of high school counselors.* Accessed at www.schoolcounselor.org/getmedia/2a38ea99-5595-4e6d-b9af-2ac3a00fa8c3/Why-High-School.pdf on August 27, 2024.

American University School of Education. (2021, February 24). *Who is most affected by the school-to-prison pipeline?* Accessed at https://soeonline.american.edu/blog/school-to-prison-pipeline on December 6, 2024.

Anderson, M., & Jiang, J. (2018). *Teens, social media and technology 2018.* Accessed at www.pewresearch.org/internet/2018/05/31/teens-social-media-technology-2018 on August 27, 2024.

Angelou, A. (2022, September 2). *Implementing high functioning teams in a PLC at Work* [Presentation]. Professional development presented for Fulsom-Cordova Public Schools at Walnutwood High School, Rancho Cordova, CA.

Arizona State Board of Education. (2022, June 9). *Social media and phone guidance for educators.* Accessed at https://azsbe.az.gov/sites/default/files/2023-08/Social%2520Media%2520and%2520Cell%2520Phone%2520Use%2520Guidance%2520between%2520School%2520Personnel%2520and%2520Students.pdf on August 27, 2024.

Bailey, K., Jakicic, C., & Spiller, J. (2014). *Collaborating for success with the Common Core: A toolkit for Professional Learning Communities at Work.* Solution Tree Press.

Banks, J., & Banks, C. (2013). *Handbook of research on multicultural education* (8th ed.). Jossey-Bass.

Biggs, J. B. (2003, March 21). *Aligning teaching for constructing learning* [Discussion paper]. Higher Education Academy.

Blase, R., Blase, J., & Phillips, D. (2010). *Handbook of school improvement: How high performing principals create high-performing schools.* Corwin Press.

Blasius, M. (2023, July 13). *How a Nintendo Switch helped locate a missing girl 2,000 miles from home.* Accessed at www.abc15.com/news/local-news/investigations/how-a-nintendo-switch-helped-locate-a-missing-girl-2-000-miles-from-home on December 5, 2024.

Brunt, C. (2022, December 22). *Racist incidents in high school football spark talks and programs*. Accessed at www.pbs.org/newshour/nation/racist-incidents-in-high-school-football-spark-talks-and-programs on August 28, 2023.

Buffum, A., & Mattos, M. (2020). *RTI at Work plan book*. Solution Tree Press.

Carskadon, M. A. (2011). Sleep in adolescents: The perfect storm. *Pediatric Clinics of North America, 58*(3), 637–647.

City of St. Charles School District. (2014). *Administrative intern*. Accessed at https://mo01910164.schoolwires.net/cms/lib/MO01910164/Centricity/Domain/51/Administrative%20Intern.pdf on August 27, 2024.

College of Community Innovation and Education, University of Central Florida. (2021, July). *A guide to the administrative internship in educational leadership: EDA one-semester internship*. Accessed at https://ccie.ucf.edu/wp-content/uploads/sites/12/2018/07/EdLeadershipInternshipGuide-1-Semester.pdf on August 27, 2024.

Common Sense Media. (n.d.a). *Parenting, media, and everything in between*. Accessed at www.commonsensemedia.org/articles/online-safety on December 5, 2024.

Common Sense Media. (n.d.b). *Parents' ultimate guides*. Accessed at https://www.commonsensemedia.org/parents-ultimate-guides on December 5, 2024.

Conzemius, A. E., & O'Neill, J. (2014). *The handbook for SMART school teams: Revitalizing best practices for collaboration* (2nd ed.). Solution Tree Press.

Covey, S. R. (1989). *The 7 habits of highly effective people: Powerful lessons in personal change*. Free Press.

Covey, S. R. (2006). *The speed of trust: The one thing that changes everything*. Free Press.

Darwin, C. (2003). *The origin of species* (150th anniversary ed.). Signet Classics. (Original work published 1859). New American Library.

Davies, B. (2004). Developing the strategically focused school. *School Leadership and Management, 24*(1), 11–27. http://dx.doi.org/10.1080/1363243042000172796

DeCourcy, K., & Schmitt, J. (2022). *The pandemic has exacerbated a long-standing national shortage of teachers*. Accessed at www.epi.org/publication/shortage-of-teachers on August 27, 2024.

Dewald, J. F., Meijer, A. M., Oort, F. J., Kerkhof, G. A., & Bögels, S. M. (2010). The influence of sleep quality, sleep duration and sleepiness on school performance in children and adolescents: A meta-analytic review. *Sleep Medicine Reviews, 14*(3), 179–189.

Dolan, R. (2022). *All other duties as assigned: The assistant principal's critical role in supporting schools inside and out*. Solution Tree Press.

Dougherty, C., & Reason, C. (2019). *Inside PLCs at Work: Your guided tour through one district's successes, challenges, and celebrations*. Solution Tree Press.

DuFour, R., DuFour, R., Eaker, R., & Many, T. (2010). *Learning by doing: A handbook for Professional Learning Communities at Work* (2nd ed.). Solution Tree Press.

DuFour, R., DuFour, R., Eaker, R., Many, T., & Mattos, M. (2016). *Learning by doing: A handbook for Professional Learning Communities at Work* (3rd ed.). Solution Tree Press.

DuFour, R., DuFour, R., Eaker, R., Many, T., Mattos, M., & Muhammad, A. (2024). *Learning by doing: A handbook for Professional Learning Communities at Work* (4th ed.). Solution Tree Press.

DuFour, R., & Eaker, R. (1998). *Professional Learning Communities at Work: Best practices for enhancing student achievement*. Solution Tree Press.

Duke, D., Tucker, P. D., Salmonowicz, M., & Levy, M. (2007). How comparable are the perceived challenges facing principals of low-performing schools? *International Studies in Educational Administration, 1*(35), 3–20.

Dvorak, P. (2021, March 4). *Not every student is Christian. So why don't all schools recognize that?* Accessed at www.washingtonpost.com/local/not-every-student-is-christian-so-why-dont-all-school-districts-recognize-that/2021/03/04/51400756-7d1a-11eb-b3d1-9e5aa3d5220c_story.html on August 27, 2024.

Eaker, R., DuFour, R., & DuFour, R. (2002). *Getting started: Reculturing schools to become professional learning communities*. Solution Tree Press.

Eaker R., Hagadone, M. Keating, J., & Rhoades, M. (2021). *Leading PLCs at Work districtwide: From boardroom to classroom*. Solution Tree Press.

Eby, K. (2022, September 19). *Free start, stop, continue templates and examples*. Accessed at www.smartsheet.com/content/start-stop-continue-templates on December 16, 2024.

Ellis, A. P. J., & Pearsall, M. J. (2011). Reducing the negative effects of stress in teams through cross-training: A job demands-resources model. *Group Dynamics: Theory, Research, and Practice, 15*(1), 16–31. https://doi.org/10.1037/a0021070

Fair, L. (2024, July 9). *Anonymous messaging app targeting teens: Read the disturbing allegations in FTC and Los Angeles DA action against NGL*. Accessed at www.ftc.gov/business-guidance/blog/2024/07/anonymous-messaging-app-targeting-teens-read-disturbing-allegations-ftc-los-angeles-da-action on December 6, 2024.

Farley-Ripple, E. N. (2012). Research use in school district central office decision making: A case study. *Educational Management Administration, and Leadership*, *40*(6), 786–806. https://doi.org/10.1177/1741143212456912

Farmer, G. (2020, August 6). *How schools and teachers can get better at cultural competence* [Blog post]. Accessed at www.educationnext.org/how-schools-teachers-can-get-better-cultural-competence on August 27, 2024.

Federal Trade Commission. (2018, August 16). *FTC provides back-to-school advice for parents*. Accessed at www.ftc.gov/news-events/news/press-releases/2018/08/ftc-provides-back-school-advice-parents on December 5, 2024.

Fermin, J. (2022, July 18). *Why role clarity is important to an organization's success*. Accessed at https://jeffreyfermin.medium.com/why-role-clarity-is-important-toanorganizations-success-5534cf0819b5 on August 27, 2024.

Ferriter, W. M. (2020). *The big book of tools for collaborative teams in a PLC at Work*. Solution Tree Press.

Ferriter, W. M., Mattos, M., & Meyer, R. M. (2025). *The big book of tools for RTI at Work*. Solution Tree Press.

Finnigan, K. S., Daly, A. J., & Che, J. (2013). Systemwide reform in districts under pressure: The role of social networks in defining, acquiring, using, and diffusing research evidence. *Journal of Educational Administration*, *51*(4), 476–497. https://doi.org/10.1108/09578231311325668

Fisher, B. W., & Hennessy, E. A. (2016). School resource officers and exclusionary discipline in U.S. high schools: A systematic review and meta-analysis. *Adolescent Research Review*, *1*(3), 217–233. https://doi.org/10.1007/s40894-015-0006-8

Fowler, F. C. (2012). *Policy studies for educational leaders: An introduction* (4th ed.). Allyn & Bacon.

Fullan, M. (1982). *The meaning of educational change*. Teachers College Press.

Fullan, M. (1993). The complexity of the change process. In M. Fullan (Ed.), *Change forces: Probing the depths of educational reform* (pp. 19–41). Routledge.

Fullan, M. (2003). *The moral imperative of school leadership*. Corwin Press.

Gallo, J. R., & Steelman, L. A. (2019). Using a training intervention to improve the feedback environment. In L. A. Steelman & J. R. Williams (Eds.), *Feedback at work* (pp. 163–174). Springer Nature.

Gladwell, M. (2006). *Blink: The power of thinking without thinking*. Penguin.

Glanz, B. (2000). Improve morale to increase productivity. *Innovative Leader*, *9*(7), 8.

Goleman, D. (1995). *Emotional intelligence: Why it can matter more than IQ*. Bantam.

Grenny, J., Patterson, K., Maxfield, D., McMillan, R., & Switzler, A. (2013). *Influencer: The new science of leading change* (2nd ed.). McGraw Hill Education.

Grenny, J., Patterson, K., McMillan, R., Switzler, A., & Gregory, E. (2021). *Crucial conversations: Tools for talking when stakes are high* (3rd ed.). McGraw Hill.

Grissom, J. A., Loeb, S., & Mitani, H. (2015). Principal time management skills: Explaining patterns in principals' time use, job stress, and perceived effectiveness. *Journal of Educational Administration*, *53*(6), 773–793. http://dx.doi.org/10.1108/JEA-09-2014-0117

Groen, J. A., & Pabilonia, S. W. (2019). Snooze or lose: High school start times and academic achievement. *Economics of Education Review*, *72*, 204–218. https://doi.org/10.1016/j.econedurev.2019.05.011

Gruber, R., Cassoff, J., Frenette, S., Wiebe, S. T., & Carrier, J. (2012). Impact of sleep extension and restriction on children's emotional lability and impulsivity. *Pediatrics*, *134*(5), e1295–e1302.

Hagel, J., III. (2021, January 8). *Good leadership is about asking good questions*. Accessed at https://hbr.org/2021/01/good-leadership-is-about-asking-good-questions on August 27, 2024.

Hallinger, P., & Heck, R. H. (2010). Leadership for learning: Does collaborative leadership make a difference in school improvement? *Educational Management Administration and Leadership*, *38*(6), 654–678. https://doi.org/10.1177/1741143210379060

Hanover Research. (2024). *Dallas ISD leverages K–12 program evaluation to maximize student outcomes* [Case study]. Accessed at www.hanoverresearch.com/case-studies/k-12-education/dallas-isd-leverages-k-12-program-evaluation-to-maximize-student-outcomes on December 6, 2024.

Hattie, J., & Timperley, H. (2007). The power of feedback. *Review of Educational Research*, *77*(1), 81–112.

Higgin, T. (2022). *Keeping your students (and yourself) safe on social media: A checklist*. Accessed at www.commonsense.org/education/articles/keeping-your-students-and-yourself-safe-on-social-media-a-checklist on December 6, 2024.

Hord, S. M. (1997). Professional learning communities: What are they and why are they important? *Issues . . . About Change, 6*(1), 1–8.

Howarth, C., & Andreouli, E. (2014). "Changing the context": Tackling discrimination at school and in society. *International Journal of Educational Development, 41*, 184–191. https://doi.org/10.1016/j.ijedudev.2014.06.004

Jones, L., Mitchell, K., & Beseler, C. L. (2023). The impact of youth digital citizenship education: Insights from a cluster randomized controlled trial outcome evaluation of the Be Internet Awesome (BIA) curriculum. *Contemporary School Psychology, 28*, 509–523. https://doi.org/10.1007/s40688-023-00465-5

Kim, L. E., Oxley, L., & Asbury, K. (2022). "My brain feels like a browser with 100 tabs open": A longitudinal study of teachers' mental health and well-being during the COVID-19 pandemic. *British Journal of Education Psychology, 92*(1), 299–318. https://doi.org/10.1111/bjep.12450

Kise, J. A. G., & Russell, B. (2010). *Creating a coaching culture for professional learning communities*. Solution Tree Press.

Knight, D. (2015). *What's "colorism"?* Accessed at www.learningforjustice.org/magazine/fall-2015/whats-colorism on August 27, 2024.

Knutson, J. (2024, September 4). *Help students fact-check the web like the pros: Build news and media literacy skills to separate fact from fiction*. Accessed at www.commonsense.org/education/articles/help-students-fact-check-the-web-like-the-pros on December 5, 2024.

Kraemer, H. M. J. (2020). *Your 168: Finding purpose and satisfaction in a values-based life*. Wiley.

Kramer, S. V. (Ed.). (2021). *Charting the course for leaders: Lessons from priority schools in a PLC at Work*. Solution Tree Press.

Kramer, S., & Schuhl, S. (2017). *School improvement for all: A how-to guide for doing the right work*. Solution Tree Press.

Kramer, S. V., & Schuhl, S. (2023). *Acceleration for all: A how-to guide for overcoming learning gaps*. Solution Tree Press.

Lang, J. M. (2010). *On course: A week-by-week guide to your first semester of college teaching*. Harvard University Press.

Langreo, L. (2023, November 16). AI is making data literacy a "survival skill" that schools must teach, experts argue. *Education Week*. Accessed at www.edweek.org/technology/ai-is-making-data-literacy-a-survival-skill-that-schools-must-teach-experts-argue/2023/11 on December 6, 2024.

Langreo, L. (2024, September 26). Students are sharing sexually explicit "deepfakes." Are schools prepared? *Education Week*. Accessed at www.edweek.org/leadership/students-are-sharing-sexually-explicit-deepfakes-are-schools-prepared/2024/09 on December 19, 2024.

Learning for Justice. (2015). *Toolkit for "What's colorism"?* Accessed at www.learningforjustice.org/magazine/fall-2015/toolkit-for-whats-colorism on August 27, 2024.

LeWine, H. E. (2024, April 3). *Understanding the stress response: Chronic activation of this survival mechanism impairs health*. Accessed at www.health.harvard.edu/staying-healthy/understanding-the-stress-response on September 17, 2024.

Li, L. (2016, December 16). Use flowcharts in education. *Medium*. Accessed at https://medium.com/@Lynia_Li/use-flowcharts-in-education-e27b5d82bb54 on December 6, 2024.

Long, C. (2024, October 17). Helping students spot misinformation online. *NEA Today*. Accessed at www.nea.org/nea-today/all-news-articles/helping-students-spot-misinformation-online on December 6, 2024.

Loyalty. (n.d.). In *Merriam-Webster online dictionary*. Accessed at www.merriam-webster.com/dictionary/loyalty on August 27, 2024.

Lynch, C. G., Gainey, R. R., & Chappell, A. T. (2016). The effects of social and educational disadvantage on the roles and functions of school resource officers. *Policing: An International Journal of Police Strategies and Management, 39*(3), 521–535.

Malik, A. S., Acharya, S., & Humane, S. (2024). Exploring the impact of security technologies on mental health: A comprehensive review. *Cureus, 16*(2), e53664. https://doi.org10.7759/cureus.53664

Many, T. W., Maffoni, M. J., Sparks, S. K., & Thomas, T. F. (2022). *Energize your teams: Powerful tools for coaching collaborative teams in PLCs at Work*. Solution Tree Press.

Marzano, R. J. (2000). *Transforming classroom grading*. ASCD.

Marzano, R. J., Waters, T., & McNulty, B. A. (2005). *School leadership that works: From research to results*. ASCD.

Masood, R. (2024, June 21). *How to help kids spot misinformation and disinformation*. Accessed at www.commonsensemedia.org/articles/how-to-help-kids-spot-misinformation-and-disinformation on December 6, 2024.

Mattos, M., Buffum, A., Malone, J., Cruz, L. F., Dimich, N., & Schuhl, S. (2025). *Taking action: A handbook for RTI at Work* (2nd ed.). Solution Tree Press.

Maxfield, D. (2016, December 7). *How a culture of silence eats away at your company.* Accessed at https://hbr.org/2016/12/how-a-culture-of-silence-eats-away-at-your-company on August 27, 2024.

McTighe, J., & Curtis, G. (2019). *Leading modern learning: A blueprint for vision-driven schools* (2nd ed.). Solution Tree Press.

Mead, M. (1928). *Coming of age in Samoa.* Blue Ribbon Books.

Mejia, J. (2022, February 1). *15 dangerous apps parents need to know about, according to law enforcement.* Accessed at https://thenationaldesk.com/news/americas-news-now/15-dangerous-apps-you-should-know-about on December 6, 2024.

Melena, S. (2018). *Supportive accountability: How to inspire people and improve performance.* Melena Consulting Group.

Michigan Association of Secondary School Principals. (2019). *Principal's checklist: 90-day plan.* Author.

Miller, N. (2014, August 20). *Twitter chats 101: A step-by-step guide to hosting or joining a Twitter chat.* Accessed at https://buffer.com/library/twitter-chat-101 on December 4, 2024.

Muhammad, A. (2009). *Transforming school culture: How to overcome staff division.* Solution Tree Press.

Muhammad, A. (2018). *Transforming school culture: How to overcome staff division* (2nd ed.). Solution Tree Press.

Muhammad, A. (2024). *The way forward: PLC at Work and the bright future of education.* Solution Tree Press.

Muhammad, A., & Cruz, L. F. (2019). *Time for change: Four essential skills for transformational school and district leaders.* Solution Tree Press.

Muhammad, A., & Hollie, S. (2011). *The will to lead, skill to teach: Transforming schools at every level.* Solution Tree Press.

Muscott, H. S., Mann, E. L., & LeBrun, M. R. (2008). Positive behavioral interventions and supports in New Hampshire: Effects of large-scale implementation of schoolwide positive behavior support on student discipline and academic achievement. *Journal of Positive Behavior Interventions, 10*(3), 190–205. https://doi.org/10.1177/1098300708316258

Nadaburg Unified School District 81. (2024). *Enrollment.* Accessed at www.nadaburgsd.org/enrollment on August 27, 2024.

National Center for Education Statistics. (2023). *NAEP long-term trend assessment results: Reading and mathematics.* Accessed at www.nationsreportcard.gov/highlights/ltt/2023 on August 27, 2024.

New Teacher Project. (2021, May 23). *Accelerate, don't remediate: New evidence from elementary math classrooms.* Accessed at https://tntp.org/publication/accelerate-dont-remediate/ on December 3, 2024.

New Teacher Project. (2022). *5 essentials for engaging families and community partners in reopening efforts.* Accessed at https://tntp.org/wp-content/uploads/Tools/essentials-for-engaging-families-and-community-partners-in-decision-making.pdf on December 10, 2024.

Nicolas, R. (2021). Monitoring productivity instead of activity. In S. V. Kramer (Ed.), *Charting the course for leaders: Lessons from priority schools in a PLC at Work* (pp. 147–161). Solution Tree Press.

Nieto, C. (2008). *Cultural competence and its influence on the teaching and learning of international students* [Master's thesis, Bowling Green State University]. OhioLINK. Accessed at https://etd.ohiolink.edu/acprod/odb_etd/ws/send_file/send?accession=bgsu1209753315&disposition=inline on December 6, 2024.

Nolan, T. (2022). *The essential handbook for highly effective school leaders: How school leaders maximize teacher commitment, engagement, performance, and retention.* Author.

O'Donnell, B. (2021, February 24). *Rise in online enticement and other trends: NCMEC releases 2020 exploitation stats* [Blog post]. Accessed at www.missingkids.org/blog/2021/rise-in-online-enticement-and-other-trends--ncmec-releases-2020- on December 6, 2024.

Office of Educational Technology. (n.d.). *Ed Twitter chats.* Accessed at https://tech.ed.gov/ed-twitter-chats on December 4, 2024.

Office of the Maricopa County School Superintendent. (2024). *Learning library.* Accessed at https://schoolsup.org/learning-library on December 6, 2024.

Owens, E. G. (2017). Testing the school-to-prison pipeline. *Journal of Policy Analysis and Management, 36*(1), 11–37.

Patchin, J. W., & Hinduja, S. (2021). Cyberbullying among tweens in the United States: Prevalence, impact, and helping behaviors. *Journal of Early Adolescence, 42*(3), 1–17. https://doi.org/10.1177/02724316211036740

Patterson, K., Grenny, J., Maxfield, D., McMillan, R., & Switzler, A. (2013). *Crucial accountability: Tools for resolving violated expectations, broken commitments, and bad behavior* (2nd ed.). McGraw Hill Education.

Peterson, K. D., & Deal, T. E. (2002). *The shaping school culture fieldbook*. Accessed at https://files.eric.ed.gov/fulltext/ED479930.pdf on December 6, 2024.

Phan, J. T. (2021, March 10). *What's the right way to find a mentor?* Accessed at https://hbr.org/2021/03/whats-the-right-way-to-find-a-mentor on August 27, 2024.

Power, K. (2021). Leading school-improvement work with intention. In S. V. Kramer (Ed.), *Charting the course for leaders: Lessons from priority schools in a PLC at Work* (pp. 11–26). Solution Tree Press.

Principal Center. (n.d.). *How to keep your desk clear with the Future File*. Accessed at www.principalcenter.com/future on August 29, 2023.

Prothero, A. (2024, August 15). Online sexual exploitation is a growing threat to kids. What schools can do. *Education Week*. Accessed at www.edweek.org/leadership/online-sexual-exploitation-is-a-growing-threat-to-kids-what-schools-can-do/2024/08 on March 17, 2025.

Rabe, M., & Jensen, E. (2023, September 6). *Exploring the racial and ethnic diversity of various age groups*. Accessed at www.census.gov/newsroom/blogs/random-samplings/2023/09/exploring-diversity.html on August 27, 2024.

Resendes, W., & Hinger, S. (2021, August 31). *Safe and healthy schools lead with support, not police*. Accessed at www.aclu.org/news/disability-rights/safe-and-healthy-schools-lead-with-support-not-police on March 17, 2025.

Re'vell, M. (2019). Toward culturally responsive: Teaching approaches. In L. Kyei-Blankson, J. Blankson, & E. Ntuli (Eds.), *Care and culturally responsive pedagogy in online settings* (pp. 148–167). https://doi.org/10.4018/978-1-5225-7802-4.ch008

Royal Society of Arts. (2010, October 14). *RSA animate: Changing education paradigms* [Video file]. Accessed at https://youtu.be/zDZFcDGpL4U?si=1nOQmfFBfGunO-Hs on December 6, 2024.

Sahlberg, P., & Cobbold, T. (2021). Leadership for equity and adequacy in education. *School Leadership and Management*, 41(4–5), 447–469. https://doi.org/10.1080/13632434.2021.1926963

Sanders, T. (2021). Taking the first five steps in high school improvement. In S. V. Kramer (Ed.), *Charting the course for leaders: Lessons from priority schools in a PLC at Work* (pp. 213–228). Solution Tree Press.

Saphier, J., & King, M. (1985). Good seeds grow in strong cultures. *Educational Leadership*, 42(6), 67–74.

Scherer, M. (2001, September 1). How and why standards can improve student achievement: A conversation with Robert J. Marzano. *Educational Leadership*, 59(1). Accessed at https://ascd.org/el/articles/how-and-why-standards-can-improve-student-achievement-a-conversation-with-robert-j.-marzano on December 3, 2024.

Schulte, B. (2018, December 18). *You can be a great leader and also have a life*. Accessed at https://hbr.org/2018/12/you-can-be-a-great-leader-and-also-have-a-life on August 27, 2024.

Scott, K., Fosslien, L., & Duffy, M. W. (2023, March 10). *How leaders can get the feedback they need to grow*. Accessed at https://hbr.org/2023/03/how-leaders-can-get-the-feedback-they-need-to-grow on December 16, 2024.

Shepherd, Q., & Williamson, S. (2022). *The secret to transformational leadership*. Compassionate Leadership.

Silversmith, S. (2023, May 1). *Indigenous student settles lawsuit against Arizona school district*. Accessed at https://sourcenm.com/2023/05/01/indigenous-student-settles-lawsuit-against-arizona-school-district on August 27, 2024.

Sinek, S. (2009). *Start with why: How great leaders inspire everyone to take action*. Portfolio.

Skiba, R. J., Horner, R. H., Chung, C. G., Rausch, M. K., May, S. L., & Tobin, T. (2011). Race is not neutral: A national investigation of African American and Latino disproportionality in school discipline. *School Psychology Review*, 40(1), 85–107.

Sleeter, C. (1997). Mathematics, multicultural education, and professional development. *Journal for Research in Mathematics Education*, 28(6), 680–696.

Sleeter, C. (2009). Developing teacher epistemological sophistication about multicultural curriculum: A case study. *Action in Teacher Education*, 31(1), 3–13..

Solution Tree. (2023, July 7). *AI conversation with Bill Ferriter and Eric Twadell* [Video file]. Accessed at https://vimeo.com/843312732?share=copy on August 28, 2023.

Sparks, S. (2020). *How we talk about the achievement gap could worsen public racial biases against Black students*. Accessed at www.edweek.org/leadership/how-we-talk-about-the-achievement-gap-could-worsen-public-racial-biases-against-black-students/2020/06 on August 27, 2024.

Spiller, J., & Power, K. (2019). *Leading with intention: Eight areas for reflection and planning in your PLC at Work*. Solution Tree Press.

Springer, C. (2020, September 28). *From theory to practice: A jigsaw approach to an elementary master schedule*. Accessed at www.schoolrubric.org/from-theory-to-practice-a-jigsaw-approach-to-an-elementary-master-schedule on August 27, 2024.

Superville, D. R. (2022, June 15). *Why understanding principal turnover is important for teacher retention.* Accessed at www.edweek.org/leadership/why-understanding-principal-turnover-is-important-for-teacher-retention/2022/06 on August 27, 2024.

TeachThought. (n.d.). *The complete guide to Twitter hashtags for education.* Accessed at www.teachthought.com/twitter-hashtags-for-teacher on December 4, 2024.

Theriot, M. T. (2009). School resource officers and the criminalization of student behavior. *Journal of Criminal Justice, 37*(3), 280–288.

Theriot, M. T. (2016). The impact of school resource officer interaction on students' feelings about school and school police. *Crime and Delinquency, 62*(4), 446–469.

Theriot, M. T., & Orme, J. G. (2016). School resource officers and students' feelings of safety at school. *Youth Violence and Juvenile Justice, 14*(2), 130–146.

Trumbull, E., & Lash, A. (2013, April). *Understanding formative assessment: Insights from learning theory and measurement theory.* WestEd.

United States Department of Education Office of Educational Technology. (2023, May). *Artificial intelligence and the future of teaching and learning: Insights and recommendations.* Accessed at www2.ed.gov/documents/ai-report/ai-report.pdf on August 27, 2024.

United States Department of Education Office of Elementary and Secondary Education. (n.d.). *Tools for engaging stakeholders online.* Accessed at https://oese.ed.gov/resources/oese-technical-assistance-centers/state-support-network/resources/tools-engaging-stakeholders-online on December 16, 2024.

United States Department of Education Office of Elementary and Secondary Education. (2024, September 20). *Keeping students safe online.* Accessed at www.ed.gov/teaching-and-administration/safe-learning-environments/school-safety-and-security/keeping-students-safe-online on December 6, 2024.

University of Michigan. (2017, August 20). *Bullying and internet safety are top health concerns for parents.* Accessed at https://mottpoll.org/reports-surveys/bullying-and-internet-safety-are-top-health-concerns-parents on December 6, 2024.

Vescio, V., Ross, D., & Adams, A. (2008). A review of research on the impact of professional learning communities on teaching practice and student learning. *Teaching and Teacher Education, 24*(1), 80–91.

Wahlstrom, K. L., Dretzke, B. J., Gordon, M. F., Peterson, K., Edwards, K., & Gdula, J. (2014). *Examining the impact of later high school start times on the health and academic performance of high school students: A multi-site study.* Center for Applied Research and Educational Improvement, University of Minnesota.

Walker, K. (2006, October 9). *Role of zero in grading* [Research brief]. Accessed at http://files.eric.ed.gov/fulltext/ED539010.pdf on August 27, 2024.

Ward, R. (2017, June 30). An introduction to education Twitter chats. *Edutopia* [Blog post]. Accessed at www.edutopia.org/blog/introduction-twitter-education-chats-robert-ward on December 4, 2024.

Wiggins, G., & McTighe, J. (1998). *Understanding by design.* ASCD.

Wiggins, G., & McTighe, J. (2005). *Understanding by design* (2nd ed.). ASCD.

Wolak, J., Finkelhor, D., & Mitchell, K. J. (2012). Trends in arrests for child pornography possession: The third national juvenile online victimization study. *Bulletin of the American Academy of Psychiatry and the Law, 39*(1), 106–111.

XQ. (2018). *Educational opportunity audit.* Accessed at https://xqsuperschool.org/resource/educational-opportunity-audit on December 6, 2024.

Zenger, J., & Folkman, J. (2014, January 15). Your employees want the negative feedback you hate to give. *Harvard Business Review.* Accessed at https://hbr.org/2014/01/your-employees-want-the-negative-feedback-you-hate-to-give on April 13, 2023.

Index

A

Accelerate, Don't Remediate (The New Teacher Project), 45
Acceleration for All (Kramer & Schuhl), 102
acceleration, 43
accountability, 121–122
    at every level, 67–76
    collaborative tasks and products, 72–73
    data-analysis protocol, 70–71
    empowerment through delegation, 122–123
    for learning, xii, 4
    relationships and trust, 122
    sample meeting agenda, 67–68
    SMART goal template, 74
achievement gap, 43
adapting to change, 4
Add-ons for Google Slides, 93
addressing concerns and feedback, 88–89
administrative assistants
    roles and responsibilities, 57–58
    weekly note-catcher and need-to-knows, 58
administrative interns
    roles and responsibilities, 61–62
agreeing on a goal, 84
"AI Is Making Data Literacy a 'Survival Skill' That Schools Must Teach, Experts Argue" (Langreo), 148
all means all, 26, 40, 49

All Other Duties as Assigned (Donlan), 59
allocating resources, 31
amygdala hijack, 66
analyzing findings, 95
Angelou, A., xi–xiii
Annenberg Public Policy Center (University of Pennsylvania), 146
anxiety.
    See reducing anxiety
Arizona State Board of Education, 154–155
articulating the why, 40–41
artificial intelligence, 132
Asana, 120
asking culturally sensitive questions, 136–137
assessing the emotional and cultural state of the school, 40
assessing your needs, 110
assistant principals
    roles and responsibilities, 59–60

B

backward planning, xii, 27–28
    benefits of, 28
    implementing, 30–31
    research supporting, 28–30
Badoo, 146
Baeder, J., 110

being honest and realistic, 41
being present and visible, 41
believers, 10, 46
bell curve, 48
benefits of backward planning, 28
The Big Book of Tools for RTI at Work (Ferriter et al.), 26
Biggs, J., 28
Brunt, C., 128

C

Calculator%, 146–147
calibrating scoring, 22
celebrating achievements, 42, 88–89
change
    implementing strategically, 139–140
    recognizing the need for, 137
change process, 2, 39–45
    changes in NAEP long-term trend, 44
Charting the Course for Leaders (Sanders), 25
Che, J., 136
City of St. Charles (Mo.) School District, 61
clarity of expectations, 116–117
coaching conversations, 161
collaboration, xii
    decision making, 136
    reducing anxiety, 116
collaborative conversations, 161
collaborative culture, 6, 8, 10–19
    creating, 3
    high school master schedule example, 18–19
    promoting, 41
    sample elementary master schedule, 14
    sample secondary master schedule, 16–17
    team agenda template, 11
    variables for master scheduling, 12
collective commitments, 6
colorism, 129–130
common formative assessments, 22
    analyzing, 23
    mini, 75
Common Sense Media, 148, 153
communicating, xiii
    creating systems, 4
    effectively, 51, 121
    expectations, 83
    flowcharts, 92
    predatory communication, 143–148
    transparently, 163
    vision, 41
    with families, 96
communication.
    See visibility and communication
community support, 89
    detailed student enrollment process, 89–92
    tools for engaging stakeholders online, 92–94
complainers, 38
The Complete Guide to Twitter Hashtags for Education (TeachThought), 94
confidentiality, 95
conflict resolution, 88
    facilitating, 1326
    steps to help guide, 95

confronting, xiii
consensus building
    facilitating, 138–139
    strategies, 136
continuous improvement.
    See reflection and continuous improvement
core values
    identifying, 8
counselors
    roles and responsibilities, 60
Covey, S. R., 29, 122, 163
COVID-19 pandemic
    changes because of, xiii
    lack of support and trauma after, 43–45
    teacher shortage exacerbated by, 60
    work of a principal affected, 2
creating a flowchart, 90–91
    example, 91
creating a professional collaborative culture, 3
creating a welcoming environment, 135
credibility, 122
cross-training, 123
    implementing in priority schools, 124–125
    importance of, 123
    research supporting, 123–124
Crucial Accountability (Patterson et al.), 67
Crucial Conversations (Grenny et al.), 83
Cruz, L. F., 39
cultivating deep understanding, 133
cultural diversity
    embracing, 4
    importance of, 128–130
culturally sensitive events and traditions, 127–128
    harmful events or incidents, 128–132
    outdated traditions, 140
culturally sensitive questions, 136–137
curriculum standards, 29
cyberbullying, 148–152
    definition, 149
    incident investigation template, 150–152
    sample policy, 149–150
CyberTipline (NCMEC), 144–145

D

Daly, A. J., 136
Darwin, C., 2
data collection and analysis, 8
data protocols, 31–33
    example, 32–33
data-analysis protocol, 22–23, 70–71
Davies, B., 26–27
debriefs, 59, 124
deceptive apps, 146–148
deepfakes, 146–148
    defined, 147
defining decision points, 90
delegating and monitoring, 115–116
    accountability, 121–123
    cross-training, 123–125
    loose and tight leadership, 116–121
demonstrating empathy, 41
designing assessment and instructional activities, 30

detailed student enrollment process, 89–90
    communicating the flowchart, 92
    creating a flowchart, 90–91
determining necessary evidence, 30
determining priorities, 110
developing a daily routine, 111
developing cross-training programs, 124
devising action steps, 84
digital literacy, 144–145
direct threats against the school or students, 143
disciplinary measures, 95–96
discussion forums, 153
division of roles and responsibilities, 52–54
documentation, 160–161
    following up verbal meetings with written accounts, 85
    of an investigation, 95
Donlan, R., 59
DuFour, Rebecca, 6
DuFour, Richard, 6, 31, 48–49, 116, 138

E

Eaker, R., 6, 27, 31, 48–49
Education chats, 94
Education Week, 146
educational equity, 43
effective communication examples, 95–99
    credit check letter template, 98
    sample letter, 97
Ellis, A. P. J., 123
Emotional Intelligence (Goleman), 66
empathy, 41
empowering staff, 41
    through delegation, 122–123
encouraging open dialogue, 138
engaging stakeholders, 41, 88, 133
    online, 92–94
engaging the guiding coalition, 41
enrollment process.
    See detailed student enrollment process
equity and inclusion, 133 modeling, 135
    educational, 43
escalated behaviors, 2
essential standards, 74
establishing a filing system, 110
establishing mentorship opportunities, 124
establishing open channels, 41
evaluating impact, 42
examples and samples
    administrative assistant weekly note–catcher and need–to–knows, 58
    building consensus around difficult decisions, 138–139
    collaborative tasks and products, 72–73
    core instructional practices walkthrough tool, 103–104
    cyberbullying policy, 149–150
    data-analysis protocol, 32–33, 70–71
    division of roles and responsibilities, 52–54
    effective communication, 95–99
    flowcharts, 91
    high school master schedule example, 18–19
    letter for a plan of improvement, 78
    letter to change high school start time, 97
    loose vs. tight decisions, 119
    meeting agenda, 67–68
    norms, 10
    principal time log, 102–103
    principal's checklist—ninety-day plan, 106–109
    priority school principal task prioritization list, 104–105
    reflection and continuous improvement, 34
    reflection on loose and tight PLC leadership, 118
    reviewing policies and practices, 137
    RTI at Work pyramid, 27
    sample elementary master schedule, 14
    sample secondary master schedule, 16–17
    social media policy, 154–155
    social media rules, 156
    staff reflection tool, 35–36
    teaching and learning cycle, 24–25
    ten-day learning cycle checklist, 25
    tool to monitor loose and tight leadership, 117
    variables for master scheduling, 12
exclusionary discipline, 52

F

Facebook, 94
facilitating consensus building, 138–139
    tool, 138–139
facilitating mediation and conflict resolution, 136
fact-checking, 145–146
FactCheck.org, 145–146
Farley-Ripple, E. N., 136
Federal Trade Commission, 146–148
feedback
    addressing, 88–89
    critical, 120–121
    importance of, 77
    prompt, 103–104
    seeking, 92, 124
    supportive, 161
Fermin, J., 51
Ferriter, W. M., 26, 132
15 Dangerous Apps Parents Need to know About, According to Law Enforcement (Mejia), 148
Finnigan, K. S., 136
flexibility, 2, 111
flowcharts
    communicating, 92
    creating, 90–91
    defined, 90
    example, 91
focus on learning, 6
Folkman, J., 121
following through, 41
following up verbal meetings with written accounts, 85
fostering continuous feedback, 42
four critical questions, 21–25, 29, 69
    focusing on, 9
FTC Provides Back-to-School Advice for Parents (Federal Trade Commission), 148
Fullan, M., 39–40
fundamentalists, 10, 46–48

G

Gallo, R. J., 123–124
gathering information, 95
generational poverty, 43
goals, 88
Goleman, D., 66
Google Sites, 94
Grenny, J., 67, 83

H

Hagel, J. III, 116
Hallinger, P., 51
hard conversations, 4, 65–67
    accountability at every level, 67–76
    high-stakes conversations, 75–85
    process for holding, 83–85
    template, 84–85
harmful events or incidents, 128
    importance of cultural diversity, 128–130
    process for addressing, 130–132
Harvard Business Review, 120
Heck, R. H., 51
helping your organization adapt to change, 4
hidden dangers of social media, 144–146
high-stakes conversations, 75
    moving personnel, 75–76
    plans of improvement, 76–83
    process for holding hard conversations, 83–85
holding everyone accountability, 84
Holla, 146
Hollie, S., 45, 56
Hootsuite, 94
how to keep your desk clear with the future file, 112–113

I

identifying a problem, 83
identifying critical roles, 124
identifying desired outcomes, 30
identifying key steps, 90
identifying low-hanging fruit, 42
identifying stakeholders, 135
image-sharing networks, 153
implementing backward planning, 30–31
implementing change strategically, 139–140
implementing consensus-building strategies, 136
implementing cross-training in priority schools, 124–125
importance of cross-training, 123
importance of cultural diversity, 128–130
incarceration, 43
inclusion.
    See equity and inclusion
increasing capacity and efficiency, 4
individualized education program (IEP), 81
initiating an investigation, 95
initiation stage of change, 40
institutional predetermination, 49
instructional cycles, 20–21
    backward planning, 27–31
    example, 24–25
    four critical questions, 21–25
    summary of work sample, 20
    ten-day learning cycle checklist, 25

tiered instruction and intervention, 26–28
interdependence, 48–49
intervention.
    See tiered instruction and intervention, 26
interventionists
    roles and responsibilities, 57
intrinsic predetermination, 49
An Introduction to Education Twitter Chats (Ward), 94

J

journaling, 160–162

K

Keeping Students Safe Online (U.S. Department of Education), 148
    key takeaways from meetings, 161
    KIK, 146
    Knight, D., 129–130
    knowing the purpose of a conversation, 83
    Kramer, S. V., xi–xiii, 2, 8–9, 31–33, 60, 102, 164

L

lack of health care, 43
Lang, J. M., 28
Langreo, L., 146, 148
leaders
    role of, xiii
leadership capacity, 41
leadership for PLCs in priority schools, xii–xiii, 5–8
    leading the right work, 7
    instructional cycles, 20–31
    data protocols, 31–33
    reflection and continuous improvement, 34–36
    norms, 8–10
    collaborative culture, 10–19
Leading PLCs at Work Districtwide (Eaker et al.), 28
Learning by Doing (DuFour et al.), 6, 31, 116
learning gaps, 2
learning goals, 8
learning walks, 59
LeBrun, M. R., 95
LinkedIn, 94
listening to explanations, 83
LiveWeb, 93
loneliness of a priority school principal, 160–161
    purpose and credibility, 162–163
    work-life balance, 162
loose and tight leadership, 116–119
    feedback and management, 120–121
    guiding coalition meetings, 120
    loose vs. tight decisions, 119
    reflection on, 118
    tool to monitor, 117
loyalty
    defined, 163

M

managing choice, 75–76
Mann, E. L., 95
Many, T. W., 6
Marzano, R. J., 20, 101–102
Masood, R., 145
master schedules, 10–19

sample elementary, 14
sample high school, 18–19
sample secondary, 16–17
variables for, 12
Mattos, M., 26
Maxfield, D., 67
McMillan, R., 67
McNulty, B. A., 101–102
McTighe, J., 27–29
meeting with staff members, 50
MeetMe, 146
Meijia, J., 148
Melena, S., 51, 121
Mentimeter, 93
mentors
    reflection with, 164
Merriam-Webster, 163
Meyer, R. M., 26
Miller, N., 94
modeling inclusivity, 135
momentum, 42
Monday.com, 120
monitoring progress
    (*see also* delegation and monitoring), 31, 42
moving personnel, 75–76
Muhammad, A., 10, 39–40, 42–43, 45–48, 56
multitiered system of supports (MTSS), 26
Muscott, H. S., 95

N

Nadaburg (Wittmann, Ariz.) Unified School District 81, 90, 148–152
National Assessment of Educational Progress (NAEP), 43
National Center for Missing and Exploited Children (NCMEC), 144–145, 147
New Teacher Project, The, 44–45, 60
NGL, 146
Ning, 94
Nintendo Switch, 147
No Child Left Behind, 43, 76
non-discussables, 57–58
non-negotiables, 116–117
norms, 8–10
    establishing, 6
    example, 10
    predetermined, 73

O

observing/tracing historical significance of traditions, 134–135
Office of Educational Technology Guide to Education Twitter Chats, 94
online threats, 142–143
    direct threats, 143
    swatting, 141–143
open dialogue, 138
OpenSecrets.org, 146
organization, 110
    assessing your needs, 110
    determining priorities, 110
    developing a daily routine, 111
    establishing a filing system, 110
    staying agile for emergencies, 111

The Origin of Species (Darwin), 2
outdated traditions, 132–134
    observing and tracing historical significance, 134–135
    process for changing, 135–140

P

pacing guides, 29
Parenting, Media, and Everything in Between (Common Sense Media), 148
Parents' Ultimate Guides (Common Sense Media), 148
parent-teacher organizations, 34
Patterson, K., 67
Pearsall, M. J., 123
perceptual predetermination, 49
personalized principal's calendar, 169–184
Pew Research Center, 148
Phan, J. T., 164
planning for supporting capacity, 42
plans of improvement, 76–85
    letter for, 78
    teacher improvement plan, 79, 81–82
PLC at Work, 3
    backward planning, 39
    four critical questions, 21–25, 29, 68
    framework, 5
    three big ideas, 6, 69
    tiered instruction and intervention, 26–28
PolitiFact, 146
PollEverywhere, 93
popular social media platforms, 153
positive work culture, 37–39
    change process, 39–45
    types of educators, 45–48
    working relationships with key personnel, 48–63
predatory communication, 143–144
    deceptive apps, 146–148
    hidden danger, 144–146
predetermination, 49
Prezi, 93
Principal Center (Baeder), 110
principals
    changed role after COVID-19, 2
    loneliness, 160–163
    role, xiii
    turnover since COVID-19, 2
prioritization.
    See time management and prioritization
prioritizing equity and inclusion, 133
priority schools, 2
    backward planning, 28–30
    loneliness as a principal, 160–163
    purpose will bring you full circle, 167–168
    what differentiates them, 38–39
priority students
    defined, xi
process for addressing culturally sensitive incidents, 130–132
process for changing outdated traditions, 135
    asking culturally sensitive questions, 136–137
    creating a welcoming environment, 135
    encouraging open dialogue, 138
    facilitating consensus building, 138–139
    facilitating mediation and conflict resolution, 136

identifying stakeholders, 135
implementing change strategically, 139–140
implementing consensus-building strategies, 136
promoting research-based approaches, 135–136
recognizing the need for change, 137
process for holding hard conversations, 83–83
template, 84–85
professional learning communities (PLCs), xii, 1–2
cultivating a network, 165
Professional Learning Communities at Work (DuFour & Eaker), 48–49
professional learning, 56, 59
project management applications, 120
promoting education and awareness, 134
promoting research-based approaches, 135–136
providing resources and support, 96
providing role clarity, 50–54
administrative assistants, 57–58
administrative interns, 61–62
assistant principals, 59–60
counselors, 60
division of roles and responsibilities, 52–54
interventionists, 57
school resource officers, 62–63
support staff, 56–57
teacher leaders, 55–56
teachers, 55
purpose
credibility and, 162–613
will bring you full circle, 167–168

Q

questions
following up with staff or parents, 161
quick wins, 42

R

racism, 128–130
achievement gap, 43
rates of referrals and arrests, 62–63
recognizing the need for change, 137
reviewing policies and practices, 137
reducing anxiety, 115–116
reflection, 159–160, 165
continuous improvement and, 4, 34–36
example, 34
loneliness of a priority school principal, 160–163
ongoing, 8
staff reflection tool, 35–36
with mentors and thought partners, 164
regularly assessing progress, 124
reinforcement, 71–72
reinforcing new norms, 42
relationships, 88
building, 122
relinquishing control, 115–116
research
on time management, 101–102
supporting backward planning, 27
supporting cross-training, 123–124
research-based approaches, 135–136
respect, 10

culture of, 8
response to intervention (RTI), 26
pyramid, 27
results orientation, 6
role clarity
defined, 50
providing, 50–5
roles and responsibilities, 120

S

Sanders, T., 25
scaffolded learning, 71–72
school resource officers
roles and responsibilities, 62–63
school social media policy, 152–153
policy examples, 154–156
popular platforms, 153
Schuhl, S., 31–33, 102
Schulte, B., 162
Scout, 146
seeking alternative solutions, 133
sequencing steps, 90
setting clear goals, 42
shared vision, xiii
sharing goals and expectations, 88
single-parent families, 43
singletons, 15
ensuring they have a team, 21–22
SMART goals, 73
template, 74
smart trust, 122–123
smartphones, 148
Snapchat, 141
Snopes, 146
social media, 141–142, 156–157
addressing effects of, 4
cyberbullying, 148–152
effects on schools, 4
online threats, 142–143
predatory communication, 143–148
school policy, 152–156
tools for engaging stakeholders, 94
social networks, 153
Southern Poverty Law Center, 130
The Speed of Trust (Covey), 163
stages of change
initiation, 40
leadership capacity, 41
momentum, 42
quick wins, 42
support, 40–41
sustained, 42
transparent and ongoing communication, 41
trust, 41
stakeholders
are change agents, 37
engaging, 88, 133
engaging online, 92–94
identifying, 135
sharing perspectives, 136
staying agile for emergencies, 111
Steelman, L. A., 123–124

strategically focused schools, 27–28
structured planning, 101–102
student enrollment process.
    See detailed student enrollment process
student government, 34
student trackers, 74–75
summarizing the current situation, 83
support staff
    roles and responsibilities, 56–57
support stage of change, 40–41
Supportive Accountability (Melena), 121
supportive feedback, 161
survivors, 10, 46–47
sustained change, 42
swatting, 141–143
Switzler, A., 67

T

Taking Action, Second Edition (Mattos et al.), 26
Tampa Bay Times, 146
teacher leaders
    roles and responsibilities, 55–56
teachers
    retention, 2
    roles and responsibilities, 55
TeachThought, 94
teams, 9
    agenda template, 12
    maximizing meeting times, 71
    monitoring, 31
    power of, 67–68
    topics, 69
teen pregnancy, 43
templates
    credit check letter, 98
    cyberbullying incident investigation, 150–152
    hard conversation worksheet, 84–85
    personalized principal's calendar, 169–184
    SMART goal, 74
    teacher improvement plan, 79–80
    team agenda, 11
Theriot, M. T., 62–63
thought partners
    reflection with, 165
three big ideas of PLC at Work culture, 6, 69
tiered instruction and intervention, 26–28
    RTI at Work pyramid, 27
Tier 1 intervention, 23, 26
Tier 2 intervention, 23, 26
Tier 3 intervention, 26–27
tight leadership.
    See loose and tight leadership
TikTok, 146, 153
time management and prioritization, 4, 101–102
    how to keep your desk clear with the future file, 112–113
    organization, 110–111
    urgent tasks, 102–110
tools for engaging stakeholders online, 92–94
    social media tools, 94
    virtual media engagement tools, 93

toxic culture, 40
Transforming School Culture (Muhammad), 10
transparent and ongoing communication, 41, 65–66
    for stakeholders, 4
Trumbull, E., 29
trust, 41
    building, xiii, 122
    culture of, 8
    in yourself, 162–163
    smart, 121–123
    with stakeholders, 87–88
Twadell, E., 132
tweeners, 10, 46–47
Twitter Chats 101 (Miller), 94
types of educators, 45–46
    believers, 46
    fundamentalists, 46
    group interactions, 48
    survivors, 46
    tweeners, 46

U

U.S. demographics, 127
U.S. Department of Education, 148
understanding the context, 40
unintended consequences, 77
urgent tasks, 102–110
    core instructional practices walkthrough tool, 103–104
    principal's checklist—ninety-day plan, 106–109
    priority school principal task prioritization list, 104–105
    sample principal time log, 102–103
using clear language, 92
using standardized symbols, 91

V

Valent, J., 43
video-sharing platforms, 153
virtual media engagement tools, 93
visibility and communication, 87–89
    community support, 89–94
    examples of effective communication, 95–99

W

Walker, A., 130
Ward, R., 94
Waters, T., 101–102
Wayback Machine, 146
Wiggins, G., 27–29
The Will to Lead, the Skill to Teach (Muhammad & Hollie), 45
working on solutions, 84
working relationships with key personnel, 48–49
    meeting with staff members, 50
    providing role clarity, 50–63
work-life balance, 162

Z

Zenger, J., 121

Acceleration for All
Sharon V. Kramer and Sarah Schuhl

Closing achievement gaps is an urgent goal for all schools, not just priority schools. The authors show that remediation is not the answer. Instead, they offer educational strategies for acceleration that will level up learning for all students, as well as a framework for implementing accelerated learning schoolwide.
BKG049

School Improvement for All
Sharon V. Kramer and Sarah Schuhl

With this practical guide, K–12 educators will use the Professional Learning Communities at Work® process to drive continuous school improvement and support student success. Target your school's specific needs with an immediate course of action for improving school culture and performance.
BKF770

The Principal's Backpack
Nancy Karlin Flynn

Purposeful self-management is key to being an effective school leader. This experiential memoir offers research-grounded tips and tools for managing yourself—so you can manage everything else. Get organized, find your purpose, know your strengths, reflect, and celebrate. This book will help you do it all.
BKG117

Charting the Course for Leaders
Jack Baldermann, Kimberly Rodriguez Cano, Joe Cuddemi, Michelle Marrillia, Rebecca Nicolas, Robin Noble, Gerry Petersen-Incorvaia, Karen Power, Michael Roberts, Tamie Sanders, and Sarah Schuhl

This thorough leadership resource offers clear steps leaders can take to turn their priority school around. Discover how struggling schools can implement a strong coaching system, create and align schoolwide SMART goals, and prioritize time for collaboration to overcome obstacles and ensure learning for all.
BKF979

Visit SolutionTree.com or call 800.733.6786 to order.

Quality team learning **from authors you trust**

Global PD Teams is the first-ever **online professional development resource designed to support your entire faculty on your learning journey.** This convenient tool offers daily access to videos, mini-courses, eBooks, articles, and more packed with insights and research-backed strategies you can use immediately.

GET STARTED
SolutionTree.com/**GlobalPDTeams**
800.733.6786

 Solution Tree